AF632212

Improving Access to Information on the World Wide Web

Improving Access to Information on the World Wide Web

Carolyn Watters

Dalhousie University
Halifax, Nova Scotia
Canada

Ess Ess Publications

Published by:
ESS ESS PUBLICATIONS
4837/24, Ansari Road,
Darya Ganj,
New Delhi-110 002.
Tel.: 23260807, 41563444
Fax: 41563334
E-mail: info@essessreference.com
www.essessreference.com

For:
SARADA RANGANATHAN ENDOWMENT FOR LIBRARY SCIENCE
702, 'Upstairs', 42nd Cross, III Block,
Rajajinagar,
Bangalore-560 010.
Tel. : 080-23305109
E-mail: srels@dataone.in

© Sarada Ranganathan Endowment for Library Science

Rs.325/-

All Rights reserved. No part of this publication may be reproduced, stored in a retrieval system, transmitted in any form or by any means, mechanical, photocopying recording or otherwise without the prior written permission of the publisher.

First Published - 2007

ISBN: 81-7000-514-0 (10 Digit)
978-81-7000-514-8 (13 Digit)

Printed at Salasar Imaging Systems

PRINTED IN INDIA

Contents

Preface

Access to information is essential to educational systems at all levels and also to society at large. In this context, Internet has challenged and made obsolete many current practices of accessing information. Web sites are now being designed and developed with greater number to deliver information for millions of users. The common browsers used to search and retrieve information, fail to give desired results, as they are not designed to handle many of the tasks. A number of technologies are now available for storing, organizing and retrieving information. Although these technologies have simplified the design and development of web sites, users are still finding it difficult to access the required information. Most of the web browsers, by design, support mostly single session and handle only simple information tasks. In her lectures, Carolyn Watters has in fact convincingly argued that most of the browsers do not provide adequate support for multi-session and complex information tasks. Whenever, the information professionals introduce a variety of information services, as a rule, to begin with they attempt to identify the information seeking behaviour, information needs and requirements of users. Similarly, before we design and develop web sites, it is necessary to identify information seeking behaviour as well as the various models of information use. In this context, it is necessary for librarians and information specialists to join the discussion on appropriate models to understand the process involved in these tasks.

While the Internet offers vast amounts of information, many of the basic characteristics of a library are missing in it. This is particularly true with regard to information organization. In this context Carolyn Watters argues that the "concept of genre not only helps people communicate, it is also useful in facilitating the match of pages to user's intent more effectively than does the search engines. "Therefore, there is a need to develop a faceted classification scheme that is extensible and robust enough to classify Cybergenre.

In her three lectures, Carolyn Watrters discussed several issues related to improving the effectiveness of accessing information in the Web. As she mentions, there are several challenges in this regard. The first challenge refers to understanding of how information seeking behaviour has been affected by Web browsers; the second challenge refers to the need for the support for complex Web tasks covering multiple sessions; and the third challenge refers to filtering Web search results in order to satisfy the user.

Bangalore
Date:

I K Ravichandra Rao
Professor and Head
Documentation Research and
Training Centre
Indian Statistical Institute

Foreword

The Sarada Ranganathan Endowment for Library Science (SRELS), founded by Dr. S.R. Ranganathan in 1961, is registered as a Charitable Endowment with the Government of India (1963).

The aims of the Endowment briefly are:

* To improve the library and information services in India
* To train library and information service personnel
* To promote the provision of efficient library and information service
* To apply research results to library and information studies

The objectives of the Endowment are:

* Furthering the cause of library and information service
* Organising Seminars and Workshops on recent developments in library and information science and the related fields.
* Organising periodically courses of lectures on recent developments in library and information science and related fields by national and international experts
* Supporting the publication of these lectures and of other nascent ideas in the field of library and information science.

The Endowment is furthering these objectives by publishing a periodical entitled *SRELS Journal of Information Management* (*formerly, Library Science with a slant to Documentation* (from 1964 to 1988), and *Library Science with slant to Documentation and Information Studies* (from 1988 to 1999). Workshops, Lecture presentations and Seminars are also organized periodically.

There are three series of lectures organized under the auspices of the Endowment:

1. Sarada Ranganathan Endowment Lectures. (1965-);
2. Dr. S.R. Ranganathan Memorial Lectures. (1973-); and
3. Curzon-Seshachalam Endowment Lectures. (2001-).

Improving Access to Information on the World Wide Web is the text of the 26th Sarada Ranganathan Endowment Lectures delivered by Professor Carolyn Watters, Associate Dean, Faculty of Graduate Studies, Dalhousie University, Halifax, Nova Scotia, Canada, during 14-16 March 2006 in Bangalore.

These lectures discuss three research issues concerning the improvement of the effectiveness of the Web for information search and retrieval. First issue relates to understanding how information seeking behaviour has been affected by the omnipresent web browser, the second issue relates to the support for complex web tasks that spread over multiple sessions; and the third issue relates to filtering web search results in ways that mirror the job of the user through the lens of genre. These are research areas with much potential to directly affect the design of web applications like the browser and to improve the ability to fully utilize the power of the web in information work.

K.N. Prasad
Executive Officer
Sarada Ranganathan
Endowment for Library Science

About the Author

Dr. Carolyn Watters received her B.Sc. in Chemistry (1970), MLIS in Library and Information Science (1975), and M.Sc.in Computing Science (1972) all from the University of Western Ontario, the London, Ont., Canada, and PhD in Computer Science (1986) from the Technical University of Nova Scotia (now Dalhousie University), Canada. During her MLIS studies, she spent, along with Dr. Mike Shepherd, a term at the Documentation Research and Training Centre (DRTC), Indian Statistical Institute, in Bangalore during 1975. They were studying in depth Dr. S.R. Ranganathan's Colon Classification and the theory on which it is based. She also lectured on Computer programming to the students at DRTC.

Dr. Watters is currently Professor in the Faculty of Computer Science at Dalhousie University and Co-Director of the Web Information Filtering Lab. She was earlier the Director of Electronic Commerce Programs for the Faculty of Computer Science (2001) and was instrumental in establishing the Master of Electronic Commerce and Executive Master of Electronic Commerce Programs. These were the first such programs in Canada created as a three-way partnership between the Faculties of Computer Science, Management, and Law, and in collaboration with five other G8 universities. She is also the Associate Dean of the Faculty of Graduate Studies at Dalhousie University and is responsible for the development of the

Interdisciplinary PhD Program which has over 60 students in a wide variety of individual programs involving all the 11 Faculties at the university.

Her research has mainly been in the field of informatics and information retrieval for over three decade. She is a member of the ACM Special Interest Group in Information Retrieval and the American Society for Information Science and Technology. She is on the editorial board of the *Journal of the American Society for Information Science and Technology* and the *Journal of Web Engineering*. She has led many workshops at conferences world wide focused on examining user experience in accessing information.

Dr. Watters is the author of over 125 refereed research papers in the area of information science and has delivered numerous invited lectures in many countries including India and China. She has also written a couple of books and softwares. She was awarded the EDDIE 1997 Software Review Award – The MathResource for the post-secondary reference category. Her current research interests include information retrieval on the Web, Web genre, and usability issue for users of small screen mobile devices. She is cofounder of a successful software company, MathResources, that creates innovative interactive mathematics learning material at both the elementary and college levels.

Dr. Watters encourages women in Computer Science and she is also interested in the historical perspectives of computing.

Dr. Watters is married to Dr. Mike Shepherd also of the Dalhousie University.

1. INTRODUCTION

In these three lectures we discuss three research issues or challenges related to improving the effectiveness of the Web for information seeking tasks. The first Challenge is to understand how information seeking behavior has been affected by the ubiquitous availability of the Web browser. The second challenge addresses support for complex Web tasks that extend over multiple sessions. The third challenge is filtering Web search results in ways that reflect the task of the user through the lens of genre.

2. INFORMATION SEEKING BEHAVIOR ON THE WEB

As the first step in developing better systems for access to the range of information now available on the Web, we must understand what kinds of information seeking tasks users are taking to the Web and how users currently perform these tasks using the tools available to them. Interestingly, the features available on common browsers, such as Internet Explorer and Netscape, have not changed significantly in the past ten years of Web usage. At the same time, the demographics of Web users has expanded from early adopters to virtually everyone; the data available has expanded from academic reports and home pages to virtually every type of document and data imaginable; the Web corpus has expanded from hundreds of thousands of pages to tens of billions of pages. We need to evaluate whether the features available in the current generation of Web browsers provide adequate support for the current information needs or do the new mix of tasks require a new generation of browser features.

The first question then is *Have we changed the way we seek information?* The answer is simple. Yes, over the past ten and certainly over the last five years, the Web has become the primary channel for distribution and access to digital information for many people. Students rarely go to the library, theses are only printed for the supervisor to read, airplane tickets are purchased online, and teenagers in North America, at least, rely on the Web almost exclusively for important information needs, such as health (Catledge and Pitkow, 1995). Almost every information need, large and small, is first checked against the resources of the Web before resorting to other channels, asking friends, finding directories, asking a librarian, etc.

The second question, *Have we changed the way we use the Web for information seeking?,* is less obvious but equally important. If we are changing the way we use the Web to satisfy our information needs then we need toexamine closely how the Web appliance, the browser, supports the new tasks.

We can categorize Web tasks by considering the motivation of the user into goal satisfaction tasks and ludic tasks. Goal satisfaction tasks are defined as tasks for which the goal can be articulated and for which the user is satisfied by the completion of the goal and include, for example, fact finding, information gathering, and many transactions, such as banking. Ludic tasks are those for which the satisfaction is derived, at least partly, by participation in the process (Dozier and Rice, 1984). These tasks are often habitual, like reading the news and generally a specific information goal can not be articulated *a priori*. This group includes web surfing, general browsing, news reading, and emerging activities such as blogging.

The Web browser does not, however, differentiate between these two types of tasks. The core tool set of the browser is built to provide access to search engines, direct access to Web pages through their URLs (typed in, history list, and bookmarks), and direct access to Web pages following hypertext links. One can argue that the search engine is not part of the browser but for the purposes of any discussion on Web use, the ubiquitous nature of the use of such services means that we must include it.

Several studies have been run over the past five years to discover the relative frequency of the different tasks in particular communities of users (Choo et al, 2000; Morrison et al, 2001; Sellen et al, 2002). While these studies are very hard to compare with each other some consistencies are of interest. First, the studies identify a relatively common set of tasks including, information gathering, fact finding, and browsing. We can differentiate these broad task categories as follows. *Fact finding* is a task for which a single page is required, where that page contains the fact in question. For example, What is the weather in New Delhi today? *Information gathering* is a task for which the user is expecting more than a single source and more than a single fact. Furthermore, the user is prepared for conflicting information to be presented and is prepared to analyze and/or compile data from a variety of sources. The task is considered to be complete when the user decides that enough data has been found to "satisfice" the information need. For example, checking out options for a holiday, writing a school report. The third broad category is *browsing* which is a good example of a ludic task, with the user often satisfied to "surf" or develop a path from Web page to Web page based on a serendipitous path, which may combine hypertext links and searches. The task is complete when the user stops, either because they have had enough of the activity, time constraint, or some other external factor.

Some studies have included monitoring and transactions as task types as well (Morrison et al, 2001). Monitoring is a repetitive information seeking behavior that may be either ludic or goal oriented and we argue that rather than considering monitoring as a type of task on its own, that there are monitoring activities that are fact finding, like checking a stock price or the weather and other monitoring activities that are information gathering, like checking a journal index, and still others that are browsing activities like checking a game site or the comics. Consequently, monitoring tasks can be considered as subsets of tasks categories rather than a unique category. Transactions, however, are a relatively new type of goal oriented task where the goal is not so much information seeking as it is information *processing*. There has been a precipitous increase in the use of the Web browser for Internet transactions such as email, shopping or balancing your bank account.

We can see this incredible increase in the use of the Web for transactions by comparing the proportion of use in 2002 study by Sellen et al (2002), which was 5%, to the 47% reported in the recent study be Keller et al (2006), shown in Figures 1 and 2.

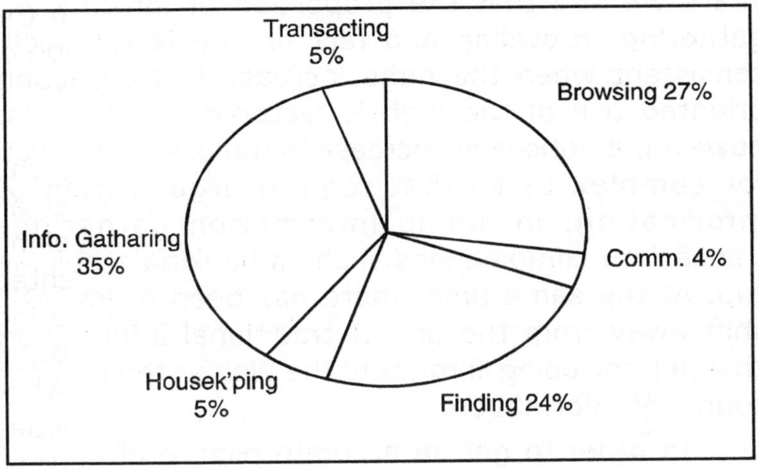

Fig. 1. Tasks in 2002 study by Sellen et al.

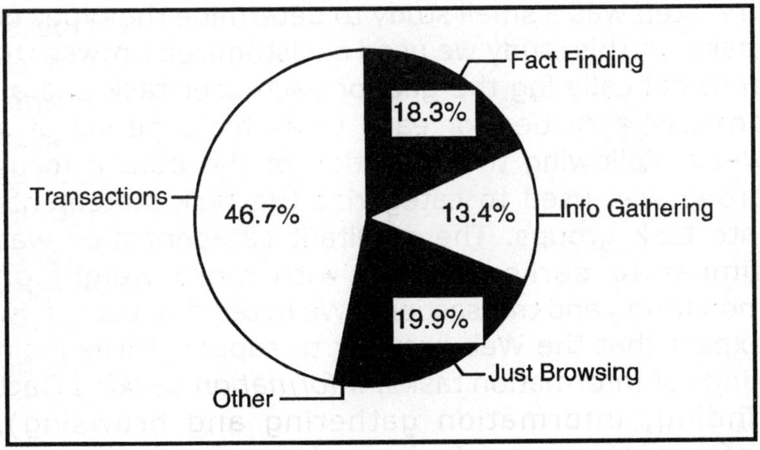

Fig. 2. Tasks in 2006 study by Kellar et al.

When we examine the trends over the past five years we see that the proportion of information gathering, browsing and fact finding is relatively consistent when the huge increase in transaction oriented use of the Web is factored in. There is, however, a noticeable increase in the use of the Web for complex tasks that require organization of information, including information gathering-transaction combinations such as booking a holiday trip. At the same time, there has been a dramatic shift away from the use of traditional information channels including libraries to the Web as the primary source of information.

In order to get an accurate picture of current behavior and task breakdown for Web users, we first examined what types of tasks were dominant and then we ran a field experiment to log how these people used their browsers to accomplish these tasks. The first step was a small study to determine the types of tasks. In this study we used a customized browser to automatically log the goal of each user task and all browser activities for each tasks for a period of a week. Following the collection of the data a focus group was used to categorize the task statements into task groups. The resultant categorization was similar to earlier studies with more weight on monitoring and transactions. We noted that users now expect that the Web browser to support three main kinds of information tasks; *information seeking* (fact finding, information gathering and browsing), *information exchange* (transactions and communication), and *information maintenance* (filling out forms, downloading, authoring, games, etc), as shown in Figure 3.

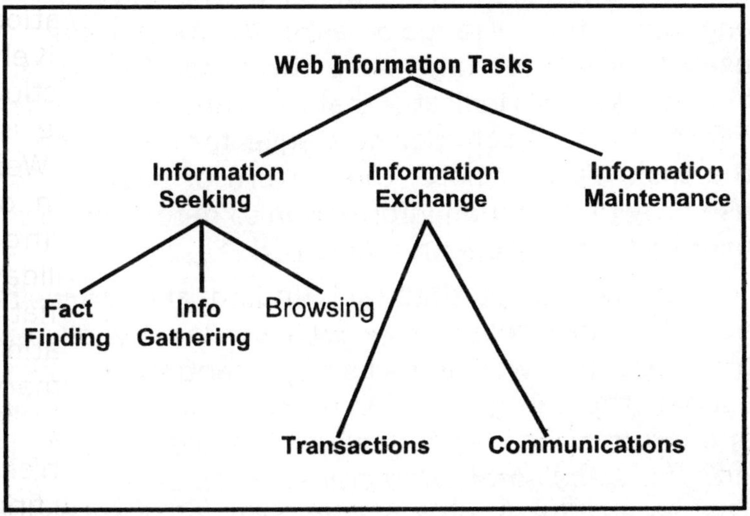

Fig. 3. Categories of Web Tasks

Using the results of the first study we engaged 21 different participants to take part in a week long field study in which all of their Web usage was logged automatically and for which the participants also logged the goal and type of each task, again using our customized browser. Using the data logged in this study we were able to catalog the relative frequency of the task types, defined in the initial study, and, as importantly, exactly how the participants used the browser features to accomplish their information goals. The results of this field study indicate that almost half of the activities are now transactions, including communications, with a fairly even distribution among the rest of the tasks; fact finding, information gathering, and browsing. In 2002 less than 5% of the activity was designated as transactions! We note that all of the participants engaged in the full range of tasks. The most frequently used browser features were the typed in URL and bookmarks. This indicates that revisiting and refinding information are common strategies for most types of the task. Furthermore, the pattern of browser tool use provided enough information to detect when the user shifted and began a new task.

If we accept that fact finding and browsing activities are reasonably well served by current browsers then we can focus our attention on how to support the new generation of information gathering and information creating tasks. The first question is, *Are the behavioral characteristics distinct to task*? That is, are the number of links followed, time spent, number of the user. If this is shown to be true then we could automatically identify the user's task and automatically provide additional support. From the field study results we noted the following behavioral patterns:

- Information gathering tasks involved longer sessions, roughly twice as long as fact finding, browsing, or transaction sections.
- Information gathering tasks involved a larger number of retrieved pages, roughly three times the other tasks.
- Users were more likely to open simultaneous windows with information gathering tasks, roughly twice as often as for other tasks.
- Each task type presented a profile that uniquely describes the use of features for that task. For example, Transactions were dominated by the

use of favorites or typed in URLS while information gathering tasks made relatively little use of bookmarks and relatively heavy use of the Google search.

The results of this study (Kellar, et al, 2006) provide some insight into the use of current Web browsers for the most common types of Web tasks. *Transactions* are tasks that are very repetitive and involve few pages. For these tasks, users did make heavy use of bookmarks, which are well suited for this purpose. *Fact finding* is a more uniquely defined activity requiring the articulation of the fact in question and a targeted search process. The quality of the experience of the user is affected largely by the ability of the user to articulate a good quality search query. *Browsing* is the archetypal browser activity that we are most familiar with, and many of the browser features, such as the hypertext link and search engine have been designed for this purpose. *Information gathering*, however, especially for complex information needs, is not well served by the current browser features. These tasks often involve multiple pages, comparison of data between pages, and organization of the retrieved information for its use.

We now have a situation then were expanding use of the Web has outpaced the capability of current browser features and new tools are needed to fill the gap. For *information gathering* tasks, which often involve access to multiple sources, the browser can support the use of multiple simultaneous pages in multiple windows by allowing the user to designate and name groups of these pages, which can be saved and reconstructed as an entity. To support the comparison of data from different Web sources, Web browsers could provide highlighting, landmarks within pages and side by side viewing of web pages. To support the organization of the information, browsers can include annotation features and filing schemes for results.

In summary, the Web is now used by millions of people for a wide range of tasks, most of which the common browsers have not been designed to handle. We are now in a position to include task in the discussion and design of new features for Web browsers. We either continue to contort the task to fit the appliance *or* begin to redesign the appliance to support our tasks.

3. SUPPORTING COMPLEX INFORMATION TASKS ON THE WEB

In this second talk we address the issue of providing support for more complex information tasks on the Web. That is, those information tasks, which typically require multiple sessions, may include refinding of information previously seen, monitoring of information, analysis and synthesis of information, and ultimately the organization and use of the results. We propose a model of user interaction called the Transient Model (MacKay & Watters, 2006) that includes such multi-session activities and we discuss the need for personal information management and knowledge management systems for use in this context.

Over the past several years the Web has taken on the role of the central large scale information resource for many people. There has been a dramatic shift of focus from personal information collection and shared library collections to the online access to all of the digital libraries and non-library resources available on the Web. Increasingly students and researchers may never use the print versions in the university library! The Web is a shared digital resource, which, unlike earlier print collections, has no classification scheme, no quality control, no library reference assistance, and no consistent archive. Furthermore, access is controlled largely by the keyword search engine.

It has become fashionable, convenient, and somewhat seductive to make all of the corporate and organizational information resources of enterprises available on a Web site. This certainly provides better access to the documents, provides more consistent updating of material, and facilitates timely remote access to shared documents. Unfortunately, making information available does not necessarily help the user complete a complex task more effectively or more efficiently if appropriate interaction tools are not available for the user. Currently, users can download or access information from the Web for use with applications, such as Word or Excel, on their desktop or server based applications may be available for remote use. If the information task, however, requires interaction over time with Web data using multiple applications, then the user has a logistic nightmare manipulating applications and changes in the Web data to complete the task.

If the task cannot be completed in a single session, then the information context must be reconstructed by the user for the next session. This may require repeating Web searches, re-following links, reopening pages, and relocating specific information on those Web pages. The use of the Web for increasingly complex tasks has grown dramatically but the development of the primary application for use of this information, the Web Browser, has changed very little over the ten years since its wide spread adoption by users.

The notion of session is important in this discussion. Let us consider a single browser session to be a period of uninterrupted activity by the user in the browser application. The user may be finding an article, reading the news, or booking an airplane ticket. The session may include opening of multiple pages, even in multiple windows, but largely concentrated on a single task. Other research (Catledge & Pitkow, 1995) indicates that such sessions last an average of about 25 minutes. We define a multi-session browsing activity as one in which the user engages in a *sequence of sessions* related to the completion of a single task. Such tasks may be time limited, such as planning a holiday for a certain date, or without a time frame, such as an ongoing interest in jazz. A multi-session browsing activity is also recognizable by two other factors; the return to previously visited pages and the collection of chunks information for later use.

By way of example, we can consider my interest in *South Indian vocal music* of special interest for my month in India. A Google search returns over three million hits from which I check out about 10 the first time. As I occasionally visit other pages I collect information on types of such music and, as I get closer, dates of concerts in Bangalore while I am there. My goal is really to have a concise reference for my use when I am in Bangalore. Once my trip is over, I am unlikely to refer to the session until a future trip to India may prompt my reinterest.

We consider two types of multi-session information seeking behavior; transient sessions and persistent sessions. Transient sessions are information tasks that are time or goal limited while persistent sessions are tasks with long term interest. Transient sessions occur either by *praxis* or by planning. Often a transient session occurs when the user's session is interrupted and the user wishes to continue again later. Other tasks are simply too complex or have time-dependent subtasks and cannot be completed in a single session. Consequently, the user plans to return in multiple sessions to complete the task. Transient sessions may, of course, be transformed into persistent sessions if the time frame or interest of the user changes over the period of the transient sessions. Similarly, persistent sessions may be reactivated as transient sessions to reflect a short term targeted information need. Figure 4 shows the inter-relationships of the types of sessions.

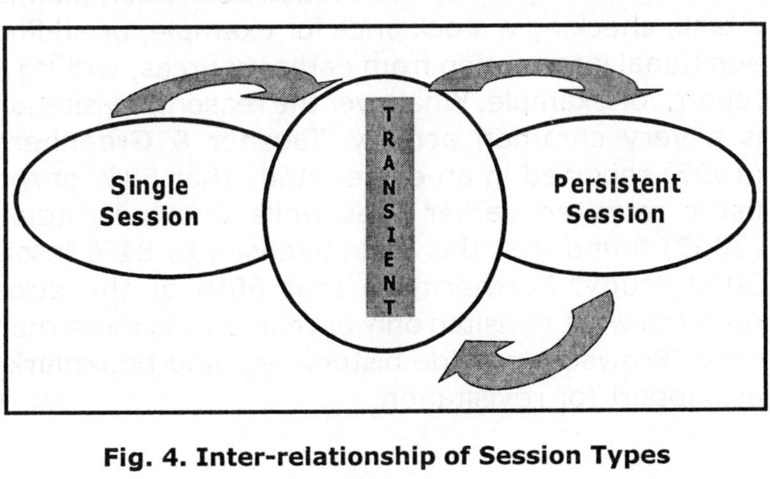

Fig. 4. Inter-relationship of Session Types

There is a relationship between the type of session and the users' tasks. For example, we can see that single sessions are suited to browsing, transactions, and fact finding. Transient sessions, however, occur where the tasks require more complex information gathering and persistent sessions fit those long term recurring information tasks that include some strategic use of information.

3.1. Session Support

In all three session types monitoring of individual sites may occur. That is, the user may bookmark a news site or a blog site of interest to check every day in a repeated series of independent single sessions. Monitoring also occurs in transient and persistent sessions and the user may bookmark sites to make it easier to complete a transient session or continue with a long term persistent session.

The revisitation of sites is a very frequent Web activity that has several goals. The user may be repeating a task, checking weather for example, or checking for some new information before completing a task, checking a stock price for example, or adding additional information from earlier sources, writing a report, for example. What ever the reason, revisitation is a very common activity. Tausher & Greenberg (1997) reported in an earlier study that 58% of the users revisited earlier sites while Cockburn et al. (2003) found that this had increased to 81% in his 2003 study. Furthermore that 60% of the sites revisited were revisited only once and 20% more than once. Browsers provide history lists and bookmarks as support for revisitation.

A history list is an automatically maintained push-down stack of sites that the user has visited based on the current session, current day, previous few days or even longer. The user can scroll down the list to hyperlink to any given page on that list. Bookmarks, however, require direct user intervention to select pages for inclusion in the bookmark list, naming of the bookmark, and organization of bookmarks within the bookmark folder structure.

Refinding is a subfunction of revisiting that involves the local identification of previously viewed information on the web page. Refinding as a task is largely unsupported in Web Browsers.

Transient sessions are defined as information gathering tasks with sufficiently large scope to require more than one session with known time lines and task goals. Typically, the tasks involved in transient sessions are multidimensional, for example, booking hotels and flights for a trip, where synchronization is necessary and may require adjustments and additions. A typical academic transient task is a three week window to find background information on a topic related to an upcoming lecture. The goals for transient sessions may, however, be more vague than the travel or lecture examples, such as, finding out something about an area before visiting or about a general topic of interest. Transient session require support for the revisitation of Web pages for the purposes of updating information, checking information, or completing transactions related to the task.

Persistent sessions differ from transient sessions largely on the basis of the ongoing nature of the task.

So for example, an academic interest in Information Retrieval would include or a personal interest in jazz may persist much longer than an upcoming conference or concert.

3.2. Browser Support

Let us consider how the current generation of web browser supports the information tasks of the current generation of Web user.

Session	*Task*	*Browser Feature*
Single Session	Fact finding Browsing	Search engine Hypertext link
Transient Session	Save results Multi-page access Resume session	——— Tabs Individual Bookmarks
Persistent Session	Restart session Manage information	Individual Bookmarks ———

We can see that browsers provide little by way of support for complex multi-session information tasks. The problem with Bookmarks, particularly over extended periods of use, is well documented; finding bookmarks in the list, organizing the list, and pruning the list. Furthermore, Bookmarks retrieve individual Web pages, not sets of related Web pages. To support complex multisession information tasks users need features that allow them to create descriptive notes and annotations for bookmarks, name and save groups of bookmarks, record bookmark attributes such as times used and quality of Web page, and bookmarks that highlight information of interest within Web pages.

Research leading to prototypes are increasingly popular. Landmarks (Mackay, Kellar, Watters, 2005), for example, have been used to supplement bookmarks by highlighting and returning the user to selected sections of the Web page rather than the beginning of the marked page. Tabs, as used in Firefox, are a feature that provides within single sessions support for users with information tasks complex enough to require simultaneous access to multiple web pages. Only Opera, however, has incorporated the notion of recovery of these tabs in subsequent sessions.

Information seeking is, however, only one step in the processing of complex information tasks. The organization, analysis, and synthesis of results from this information are a critical part of Web information tasks and are largely ignored by browsers. The user may download pages, save links, print pages, cut and paste sections for use in other management applications but not within the browser. Research into Personal Information Management (PIM) models has a rich history that has implications for design in browsers. Research in the PIM area indicates that users will avoid complex filing schemes if possible. Information available through the browser includes three types; short shelf life information such as a news article, in progress information useful during the course of the task such as a report, and archival information useful over a longer period such as an academic background search. It remains an open question how to support the need of users to integrate their web data with their other information storage schemes.

3.3. Summary

The current generation of web browsers supports single session and relatively simple information tasks quite well. These browsers do not, however, provide adequate support for multi-session and complex information tasks that go past simple retrieval of information. Before we design or evaluate new tools for this context, models of information use are needed. Librarians and information specialists should join the discussion of appropriate models to understand the process involved in these tasks and from that perspective join in the design of new tools for the user.

A final philosophical discussion arises from how to integrate local and remote information processing. That is, should we move the Web search functions out from the Web browser and into the other information processing applications or should we expand the capabilities of the web Browser into the universal Web information managing appliance?

4. GENRE AND INFORMATION SEEKING ON THE WEB

In the final talk we address the issue of categorizing Web search engine results post search for the user. The use of the search engine for the identification of potential resources on the Web for a variety of information seeking tasks has replaced almost all other access methods to digital resources. The suitability of such a gross tool for individual information requests is under considerable debate. There are currently different approaches to this problem. The first is a renewed interest in ontologism for domains, including both semantic web initiatives and Yahoo style directories. The second approach is to develop pre and post search filters to processing the results of the generic search engine to better match the needs of the user.

In this talk we examine the potential role of genre in the categorization of search results to filter results by type of document to better approximate the intent of the user in accessing the document.

4.1. Genre and Cybergenre

Genre has been used since Aristotle to classify types of discourse. Most classification schemes base genre on the notion of rhetorical style (Miller, 1984), for example, the essay, poem or novel. Yates and Orlikowski (1994) introduced the broader notion of genre based on socially recognized communicative purpose within organizational structures, examples being the memo or financial statement. We will use the generally accepted concept of genre as characterized by the combination of form and content as a social construct with communicative purpose.

In the context of the digital media of the Web, genre takes on new significance. The media affords functionalities not existing in earlier channels that dramatically affect the usefulness and purpose of existing genre and, furthermore, support new genre only possible in this media. We define such Web based genre as Cybergenre (Shepherd and Watters, 1998) and highlight the importance of functionality in genres occurring on the Web.

Let us take a look at the Web version of the news paper. We recognize the web page as an instance of the newspaper genre largely on the content and form as presented. That is, it looks like a newspaper and meets the expectations of a newspaper for the reader. It has sections, advertisements, headlines, broadsheet layout, current stories, etc. The Web version, however, comes with the potential of added functionality; dynamically updated headlines, shopping, online discussions, active crosswords and puzzles, video clips, keyword search, etc.

The news is only one example of the affordance provided by the Internet channel on genre. There is a predictable and ongoing evolutionary pattern to genre taken from an earlier media and transported to the new media. On the Web we find that first examples of Web genre are simply reproduction of print genre and then as new functionality is exploited until the cyber version may no longer be entirely recognizable as the original. At the same time, completely new and novel genres appear on the new media as a response to the new capabilities afforded. The FAQ (Frequently asked Question) pages and home pages are two examples of novel cyber genre that have appeared spontaneously on the Web.

While search engines provide access to over 10 billion pages on the Web, users are reluctant to use more than 3 terms to find relevant material. Not surprisingly, for most information seeking tasks, users are not satisfied by the gross matching that occurs in this context at the search engine level. The user is no longer faced with a retrieval problem but rather is now faced with a *selection* problem. The success of coarse grained keyword searches that function reasonably well in small corpora has been lost in the sheer scale of the Web resources. Users need less not more information. The problem then is how to help the user be more selective in accessing the results of these searches on the Web. One solution would be to help users articulate perfect or at least much more precise search queries. The other solution, the focus of this talk, is to help users by categorizing the results to facilitate more effective selection from the hit set.

We propose the use of classification of search engine results based on the Cybergenre as a tool to help the user match the intent of the query with the type of document expected to be most useful for that task. For example, if a user is trying to buy a car he or she may be interested in car reviews or car sales but likely not academic studies of cars or joke pages about cars. If a query produces a large hit set of documents that satisfy the query, the genre of the documents could be used to dynamically group the results into genre, perhaps home pages, academic reports, corporate pages, or shopping sites, depending on the user's needs. The user could then focus on the type of document he or she considers to be best suited to their current task. Figure 5 shows an example prototype of this type of interest working on Google results.

The difficulty is, of course, identification of the genre of given web pages. Again, we can restrict our discussion to known domains or collections but that is, arguably, not the reality of searching on the Web or we can examine the potential for automatic identification of cybergenre.

4.2. Definition of Cybergenre Attributes

How then can we identify cybergenre, especially in light of the fast evolutionary trends exhibited on the Web over the past 10 years? We propose the

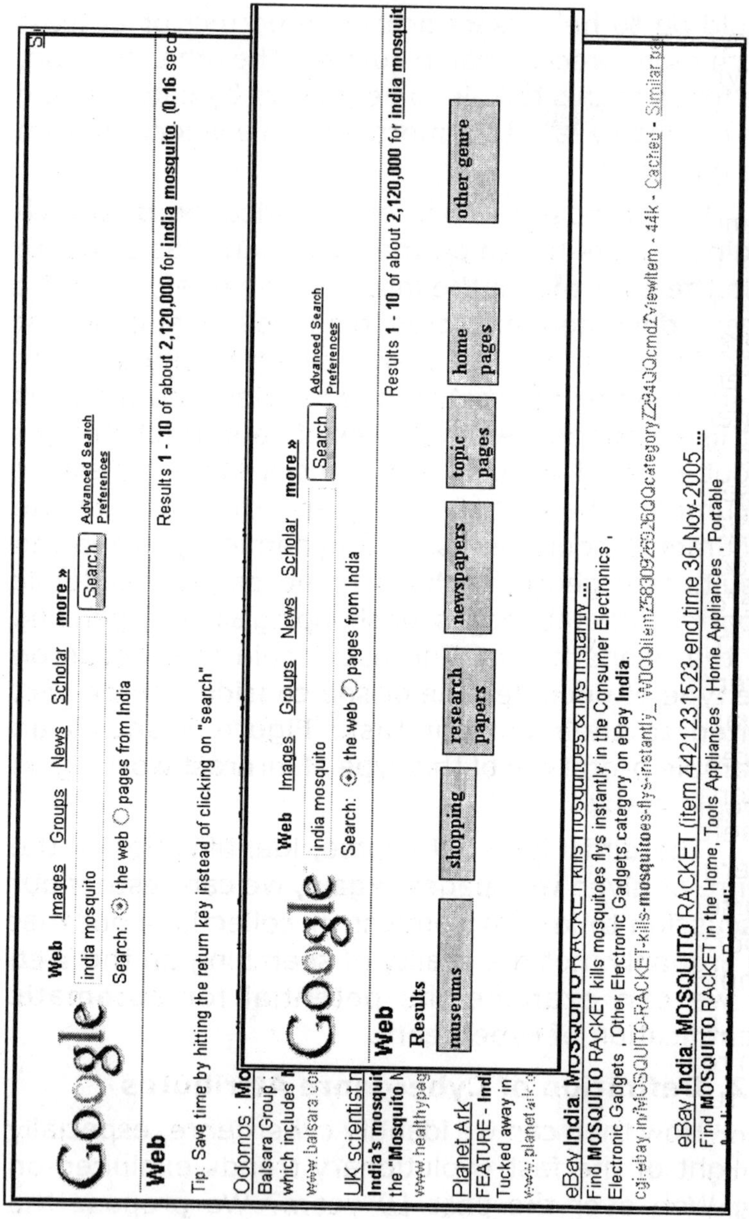

Fig. 5. Sample Post Processing of Google Search by Genre

following feature set based on the general definition of cybergenre:

Content (keywords & metadata, source, date)

Form (structure, style, language level, length, data types)

Functionality (scripts, dynamic generation, links, communication types)

Purpose (intended audience).

The first problem is to define the cybergenre of interest to users within the context of the user's current task. That leads to the discussion of generating a catalog of existing cybergenres. The second problem is to consider what features we can use to identify those genres automatically and dynamically. The third problem, likely the most difficult of the three, is how to recognize new and evolving cybergenres as they emerge.

There is little if no agreement on a catalog of current genre on the Web. Attempts have resulted in upwards of 1000 different and slightly different genres. Rather than attempt to catalog definitively current variations of all cybergenre we have chosen to select a few well recognized and well used Cybergenres that may be useful for categorizing user Web search results, such as the personal home page, corporate pages, academic reports, FAQs, blogs, and shopping catalogs.

Using the textual content of Web pages, we have been reasonably successful in identifying home pages and further in identifying personal home pages, corporate, and organizational home pages using very few features (Shepherd et al, 2004). Figure 6 shows the small set of content features that can be used successfully for this purpose.

Content Features Used	
Class	Terms
Personal Home Page	my, me, i, t
Corporate Home Page	we, services, service, available, fax, our, us, com, contact, copyright, free, amp
Organization Home Page	events, community, organization, 2004, help, its, members, news, information

Fig. 6. Content features used to identify sub-genres of Home Pages

In a second study (Zhang et al, 2006) we again used content features to identify shopping style pages, health pages, and educational pages, with reasonably good results. Web pages which had little text were, however, difficult to identify using this method. In Figure 7, we can see the separation onto three dimensions of the three genres.

The outstanding research questions then include:

* What is the appropriate feature set for identifying genres?
* What is the relative weight of features derived from content, form and functionality?

4.3. Genre Classification

There is an intuitive appeal to developing ontology of cybergenre that could be used in classifying Web pages and in recognizing new genre as they emerge. Such a scheme would need to work across domains unlike many of the current such schemes that provide a classification within domains.

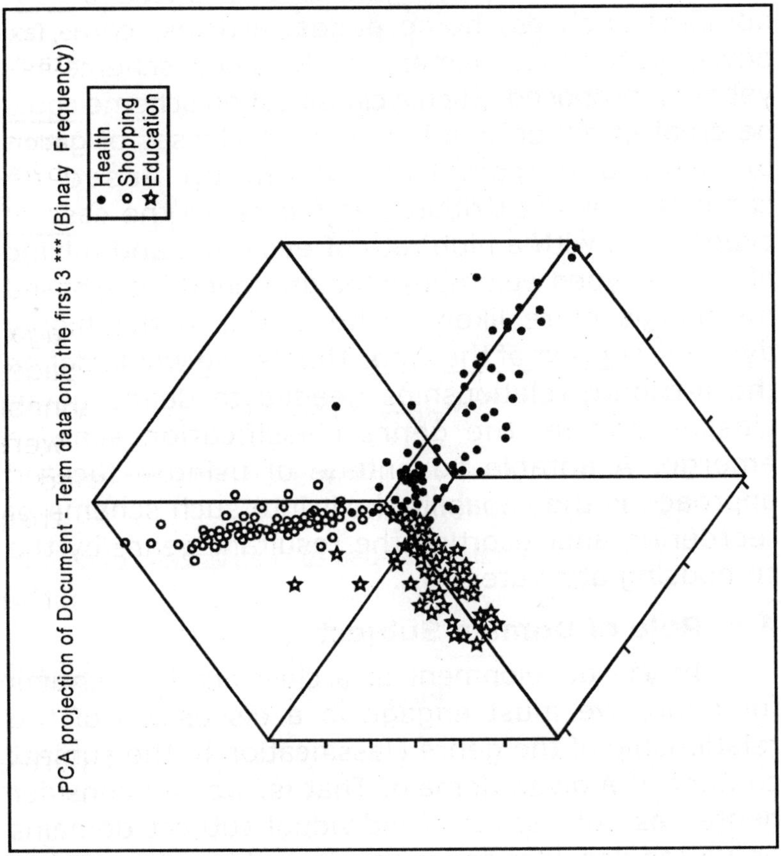

Fig. 7. Identification of Health, Shopping, and Educational Genres

For example, within Belles Lettres (800) in the Dewey Decimal System we find English poetry (821), English drama (822), English fiction (823), and English speeches (825). An examination of Web pages reveals broad classes of page genres distributed across domains such as; home pages, articles, catalogs, news, dictionaries, games, etc. No single schema has yet been proposed. Such a classification scheme could be created either as a hierarchy of classes of genre or grounded from the bottom up based on combinations of attributes as facets. In the case of cybergenre with a high rate of evolution and mixing of genres types we propose the grounded facet-based method is more likely to be useful in the highly dynamic context of the Web. That is, we would define the attribute relationships needed to define genre classes and let the genre classification scheme emerge. A notable advantage of using a faceted approach is the capability built into such schema of reordering and resorting the resultant genre by the composing attributes.

4.4. Role of Domain Subject

In the development of a classification scheme for genre we must engage in a discussion of the relationship of the genre classification to the subject content of a given domain. That is, we can consider genres as subclasses of individual subject domains or we can consider genre as overarching classes that may apply across subject domains. Figure 8 shows the relationship of these organizational concepts.

Two Level Approach to Use	
* **By Subject** - Medicine - Sports - Science - Politics - Entertainment - Computers	* **By Genre/Type** - Reviews - Blogs - Scholarly articles - Home pages - News - Editorial articles - Sports scores

Fig. 8. Categorization by Subject vs. Categorization by Genre

The usefulness of this question lies in where we plan to apply the concept of genre. If we intend to metatag pages by subject specific genre then the user could specify "I want home pages for companies making laptops" and this information can be used pre search by the search engine to restrict the scope of the search. This unfortunately only works if all Web resources are appropriately tagged! On the other hand, if we consider the concept of genre as a post search organizing strategy, then the results for a search "companies making laptops" may be presented as the set of home pages, a set of catalogs, a set of financial statements, and a set of news articles.

4.5. Summary

Just as the concept of genre helps people communicate, the concept of genre may be useful in facilitating the match of

pages to user's intent more effectively than does the search engine. One of the core difficulties is understanding the classes of genre existing on the Web currently and proposing a classification scheme that would allow for integration of genre into the search process. We challenge the Indian Classification experts, in particular, to give serious thought to the development of a faceted classification scheme that is extensible and robust enough to classify Cybergenre. We do not underestimate this challenge but are convinced that this is the way forward in organizing search results for real users.

5. CONCLUSION

In these three talks we have discussed three challenges related to improving the experience of users with information seeking tasks on the Web. The first challenge is to understand how the browser supports information seeking tasks. The second is related to understanding more complex multi-session Web tasks and the final challenge is to consider the role of genre in this context. These are very exciting research areas with huge potential to directly affect the design of Web appliances, such as the browser, and to vastly improve the ability of users to fully utilize the power of the Web in information tasks.

Finally, I would like to thank the Sarada Ranganathan Endowment for the honour of inviting me to present the Endowment lectures for 2006. My association with DRTC and Indian colleagues, which started from my first visit in 1975, has been long and fruitful. I am indebted in so many ways to the friendship, collegiality, and academic stimulation that I have found and continue to find within in this community.

REFERENCES

1. Catledge, L. D. and Pitkow, J. E. 1995. Characterizing Browsing Strategies in the World-Wide Web. **In** *Proc. of WWW 1995*, Darmstadt, Germany, 1065 - 1073.
2. Choo, C. W., Detlor, and Turnbull, D. 2000. Information Seeking on the Web: An Integrated Model of Browsing and Searching. *First Monday*, 5(2).
3. Cockburn, A. S.; Greenberg, S.; Jones, B.; McKenzie, and M. Moyle. 2003. Improving Web Page Revisitation: Analysis, Design, and Evaluation. *Information Technology and Society: Special Issue on Web Navigation*. 3(1); 159-183.
4. Kellar, M.; C.Watters and M. Shepherd. A Field Study Characterizing Web-based Information Seeking Tasks. Accepted to *Journal of the American Society for Information Science and Technology*. 2006.
5. MacKay, B.; Kellar, M. and Watters, C. An Evaluation of Landmarks for Re-Finding Information on the Web. In *Proc. of CHI 2005*. Portland, Oregon. 2005
6. MacKay, B. and C.Watters. Transient Web Model. Technical Report. Dahousie University, Faculty of Computer Science, 2006.
7. Miller, C. R. Genre as Social Action. *Quarterly Journal of Speech*, 70, 1984, 151-176.
8. Morrison, J.; Pirolli, P. and Card, S. A taxonomic analysis of what world wide web activities significantly impact people's decisions and actions. **In** *Proc of CHI 2001*. 2001, 163-164.
9. Dozier, D. and Rice, R. Rival Theories of Electronic Newsreading. In R. Rice, (Ed.), *The new media* (pp. 103-128). London: Sage Publications, 1984.
10. Sellen, A. J.; Murphy, R. and Shaw, K. L. How Knowledge Workers Use the Web. In *Proceedings of CHI 2002*, Minneapolis, MN. 2002, 227- 234
11. Shepherd, M. and C. Watters. The Evolution of Cybergenre. Proceedings of *Thirty-First Annual Hawaii International Conference on System Sciences-Volume 2*, 1998.
12. Shepherd, M.; Watters, C. and A. Kennedy. Cybergenre: Automatic Identification of Home Pages on the Web. *Journal*

of Web Engineering, Vol. 3(3&4), 2004, 236-251.

13. Tausher, L. and S. Greenberg. Revisitation Patterns in World Wide Web Navigation Revisitation Patterns in World Wide Web Navigation. **In** *Proceedings of the CHI '97 Conference.* 1997.
14. Yates, J. and Orlikowski, W. Genres of Organizational Communication: A Structurational Approach to Studying Communication and Media. *Academy of Management Review,* 17(2), 1992, 299-326.
15. Zhang, R.; M. Shepherd; J. Duffy, and C. Watters (2006). Automatic Web Page Categorization using Principal Component Analysis. Accepted at the HICSS Conference, 2007.

Power Point Presentation Slides

Challenges

* Challenge I: What information tasks are people now doing on the web?
* Challenge II: How to support complex information task behavior on Web?
* Challenge III: How to categorize Web search results to support tasks?

Slide 1

Challenge I :

What information tasks are people now doing on the web?

Slide 2

Information Seeking Behaviour on the

WEB

"You can't manage what you don't measure"
Peter Drucker

Melanie Kellar

Slide 3

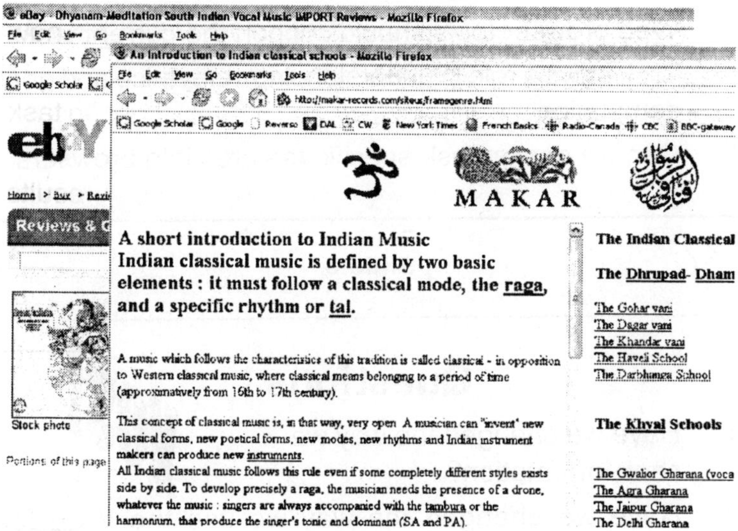

Slide 4

Web Users and Tasks

* What do people use the Web for?
* Has this changed since earlier studies?
* [How does this differ from the use of traditional print?]
* What browser features are used for different user goals?

Slide 5

Motivation

* Web browser tools should support the <u>current</u> tasks

* Task plays a role in understanding relevance and goal completion

* Can we design task-specific features into browsers

Slide 6

Questions

yes!

1. Have we changed the way we seek information?
2. Have we changed the way we use the Web for information seeking?

Slide 7

Tasks & Tools

Tasks

Fact Finding **Information Gathering**	} **Goal oriented**
Transactions	
Browsing	} **Ludic**
Communication	

Tools

Web browser & search engine

Slide 8

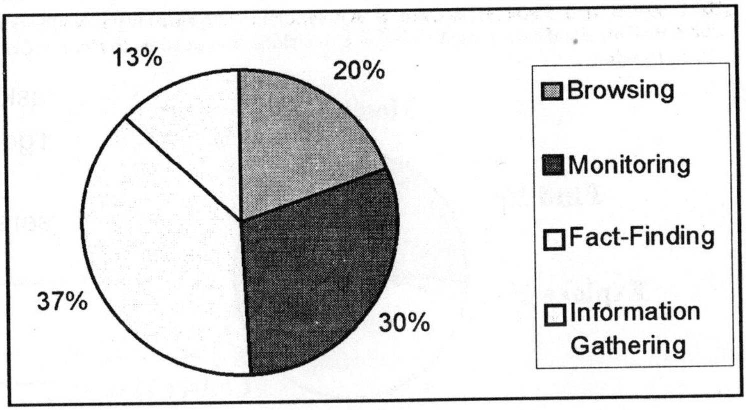

Slide 9

2002. Sellen, A. J., Murphy, R., and Shaw, K. L. How Knowledge Workers Use the Web. In *Proceedings of CHI 2002,* Minneapolis, MN. 227- 234

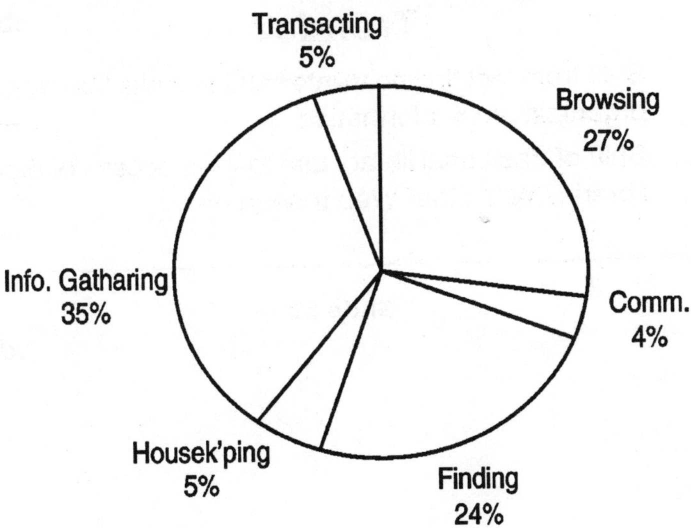

Over half of activities recognizable as information seeking

Slide 10

2001. Morrison, J. Pirolli, P., & Card, S. A taxonomic analysis of w hat world wide web activities significantly impact people's decisions and actions. In *Proc of CHI 2001. 163-164.*

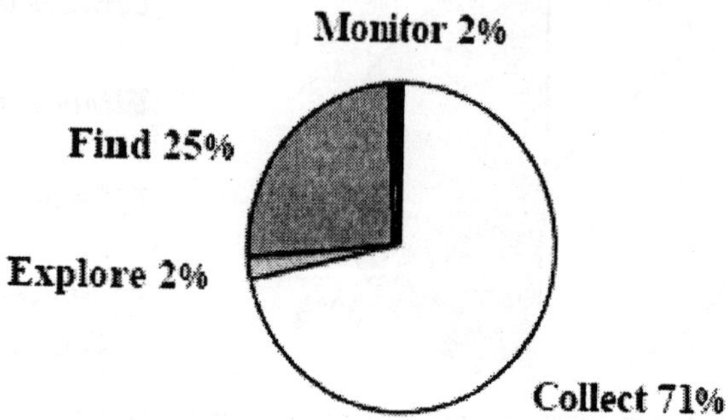

Slide 11

Trends?

* Shift from fact finding to information tasks that require organization of information
* Shift of traditional library use to Web access of digital libraries plus other Web resources

Slide 12

Slide 13

What are we doing now on the Web?		
* Pilot study	Looking for some participatory design references	Looking for C# reference material
* Collected users task statements over a week	Looking for the Super bowl score	Downloading a piece of software
* Focus group to categorize statements	Finding percentage of population that is left handed	Looking for a recipe for pizza dough
	Trying to find a reviewer for a conference paper	Looking for things to do in Paris

Slide 14

Resulting Task Categories

- Fact Finding
- Information Gathering
- Browsing
- Monitoring*
- Transactions
- "Other"

Slide 15

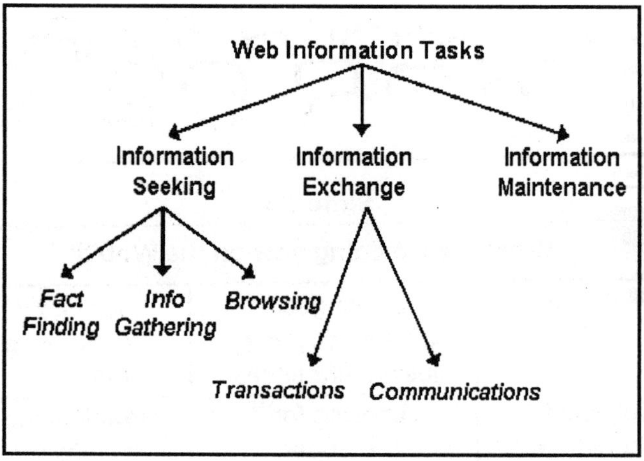

Slide 16

Web Use Field Study Design

- 21 participants took part in a one week study logging all of their behaviour on the Web
- Pre and post session questionnaires

Slide 17

Collecting Data

* Explicit statement of task

— What is the goal?

* Implicit Logging of data within task

— What queries? What sites? What tools?

Slide 18

Getting Task Information

Slide 19

Diary method

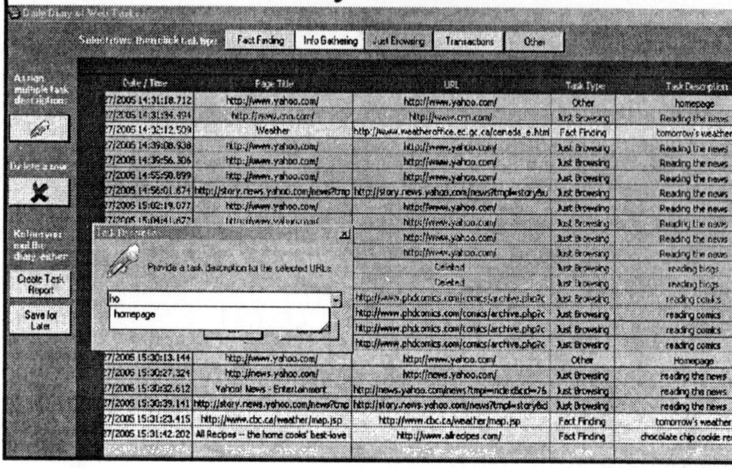

Slide 20

Data Capture

Task Data

WINDOW_ID, DATE_TIME, PAGE_TITLE, URL, TASK_TYPE TASK_DESCRIPTION
26229,8/14/2005 18:03:48.018,MSN.com,http://www.msn.com/,Other, homepage
26229,8/14/2005 18:04:12.273, Local Weather Page,http://www.weather.com/<snip>, Fact Finding, weather
26229,8/14/2005 18:04:40.965,CNN.com,http://www.cnn.com/, Just Browsing, news
26229,8/14/2005 18:05:41.812,Travelocity, http://www.travelocity.com/, Info Gathering, plan trip
26229,8/14/2005 18:05:48.572,Guides & Advice,http://dest.travelocity.com/<snip>, Info Gathering, plan trip

Browser Feature Data

WINDOW_ID, DATE_TIME, PAGE_TITLE, URL,FUNCTION, DESCRIPTION
26229,8/14/2005 18:03:41.139,title,url,Browser_Function,OPEN_SESSION
26229,8/14/2005 18:03:48.039,title,url,Document_Complete,FIRST_PAGE
26229,8/14/2005 18:04:12.404,title,url,Document_Complete,FAVORITES_TOOLBAR
26229,8/14/2005 18:04:40.985,title,url,Document_Complete,ENTER_KEY
26229,8/14/2005 18:05:25.659,title,url,Browser_Function,PASTE_COMBO
26229,8/14/2005 18:05:41.832,title,url,Document_Complete,GO_BUTTON
26229,8/14/2005 18:05:48.582,title,url,Document_Complete,CLICKED_LINK
26229,8/14/2005 18:05:52.337,title,url,Browser_Function,CLOSE_SESSION

Slide 21

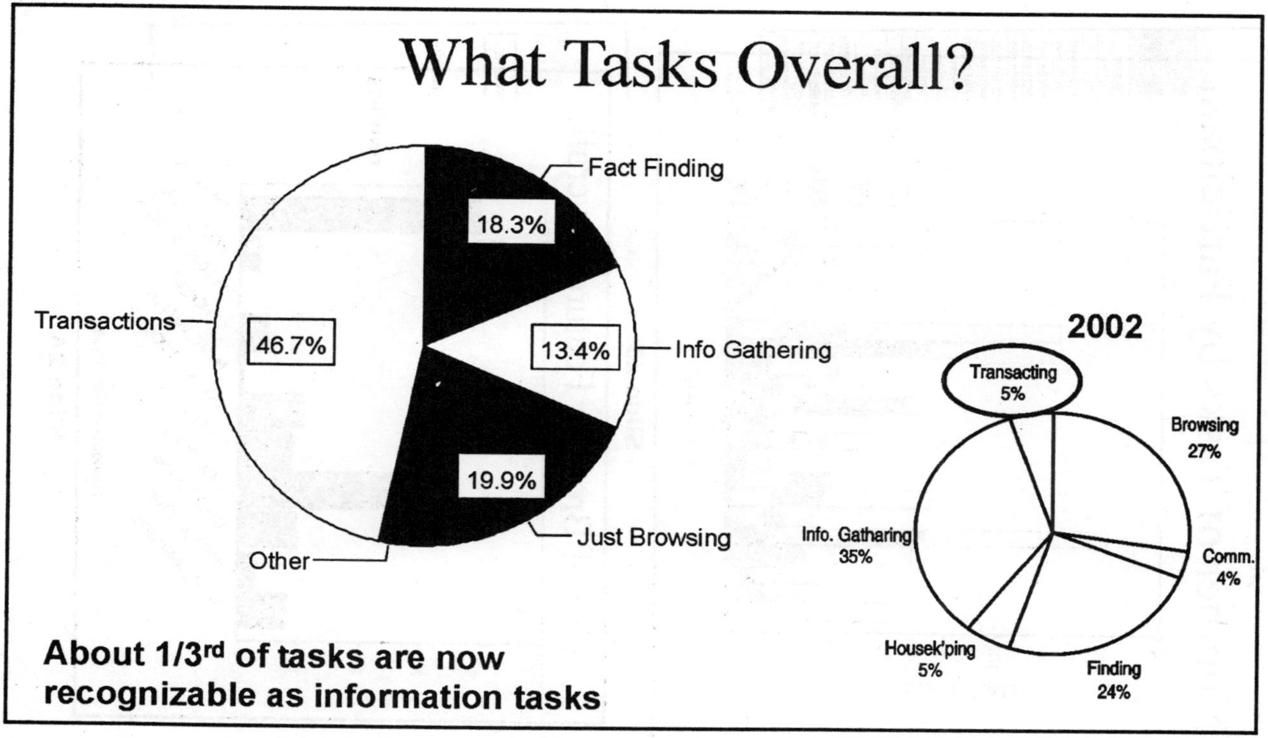
What Tasks Overall?
Fact Finding
18.3%
Transactions
46.7%
13.4%
Info Gathering
19.9%
Just Browsing
Other
About 1/3rd of tasks are now recognizable as information tasks
2002
Transacting 5%
Browsing 27%
Info. Gatharing 35%
Comm. 4%
Housek'ping 5%
Finding 24%

Slide 22

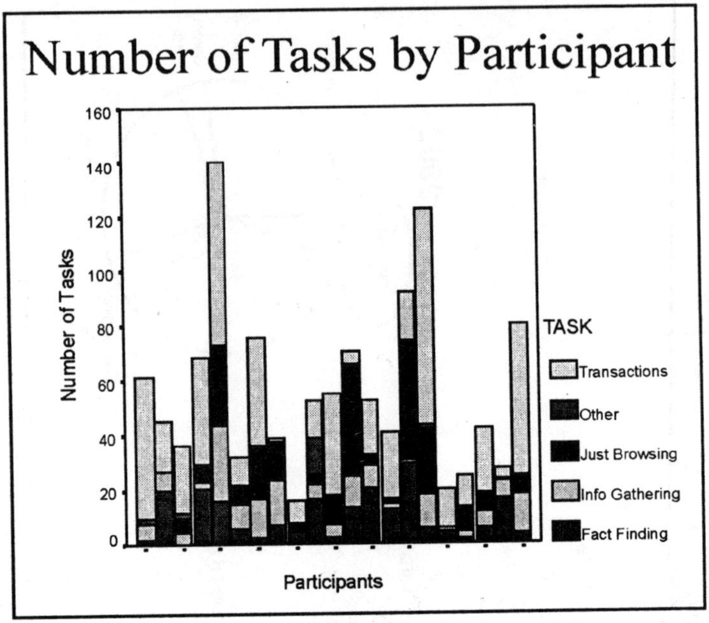

Slide 23

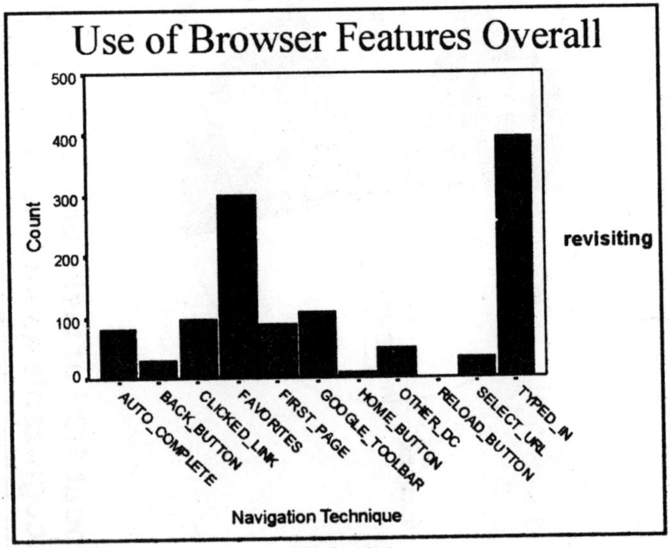

Slide 24

Use of Features To <u>Initiate</u> New Task

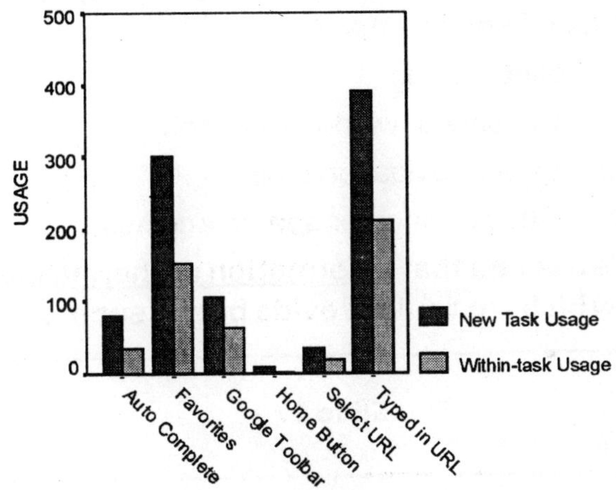

Slide 25

Hammer problem

* When I only have a hammer, everything is a nail

* When I only have a browser, everything is a search or link

Slide 26

How is the browser used for Tasks?

- * Are there behavioural characteristics that distinguish one task from the other?
- * Time spent reading
- * Number of pages, windows opened
- * Web browser navigation tools
- * Use of Google (or other search engines)
- * **Let's assume that <u>Information gathering</u> is a task for which we could provide better support!**

Slide 27

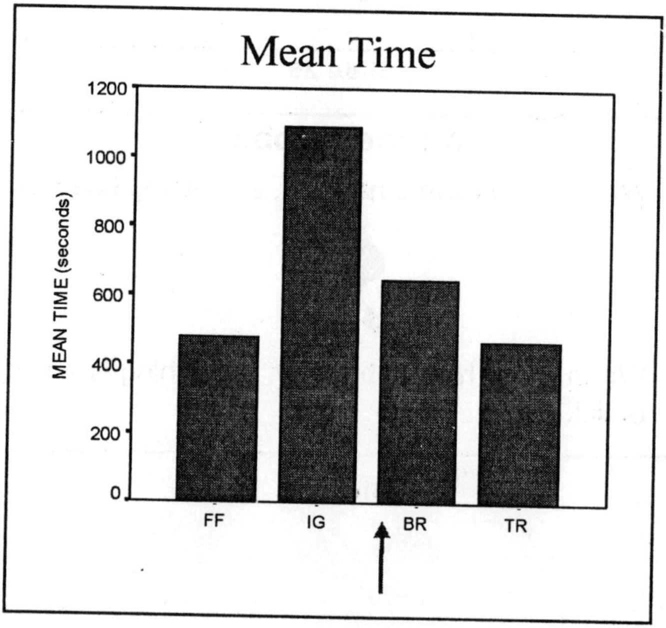

Slide 28

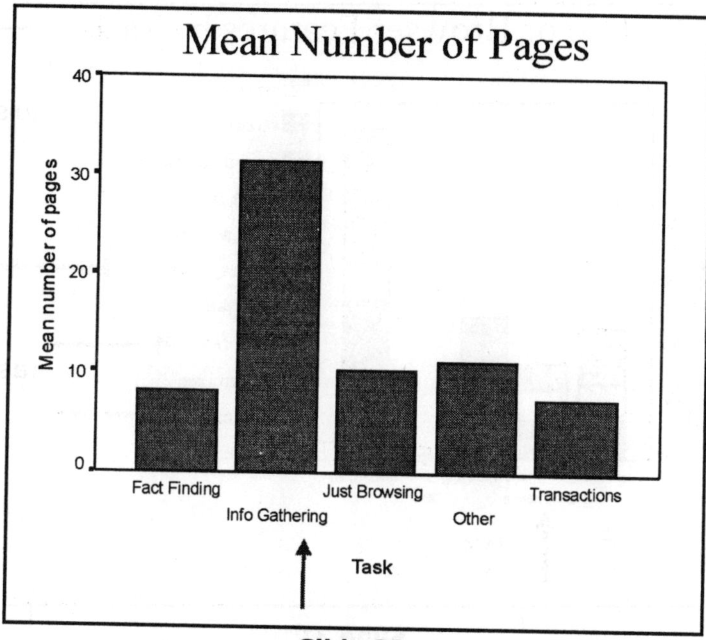

Slide 29

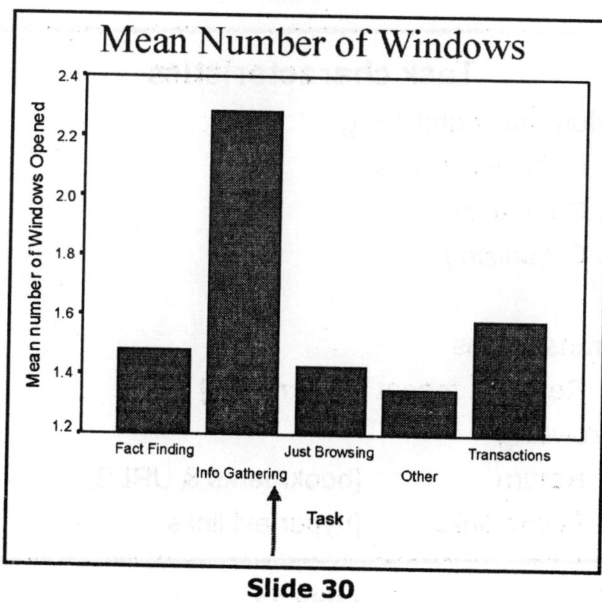

Slide 30

Use of Browser Features by Task

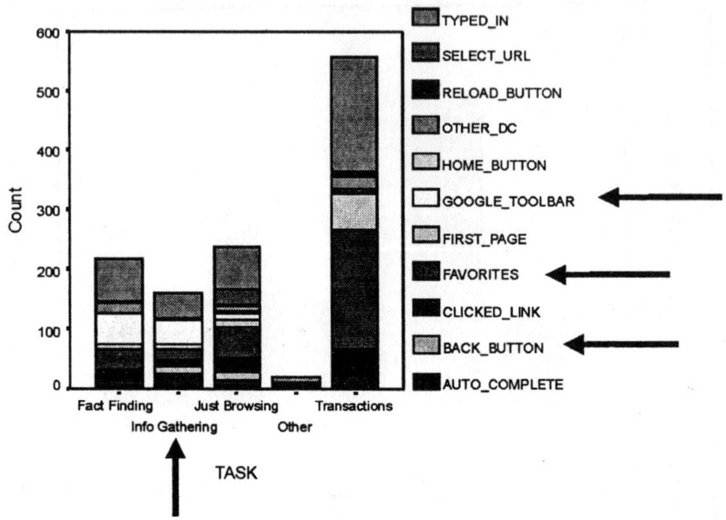

Slide 31

Task characteristics

* Information gathering

1. Multiple sources
2. Comparing
3. Organizing

* Transactions

– Return & repeat [bookmarks]

* Browsing

– Return [bookmarks & URLS]

– Follow links [hypertext links]

Slide 32

Potential Browser Support

* Information gathering
  * Multiple sources
    - Multiple pages
    - Multiple windows
    - Notion of grouping
  * Comparing
    - Side by side viewing
    - Creating result page
    - Landmarks
  * Organizing
    - Annotation & Metadata
    - Filing

Slide 33

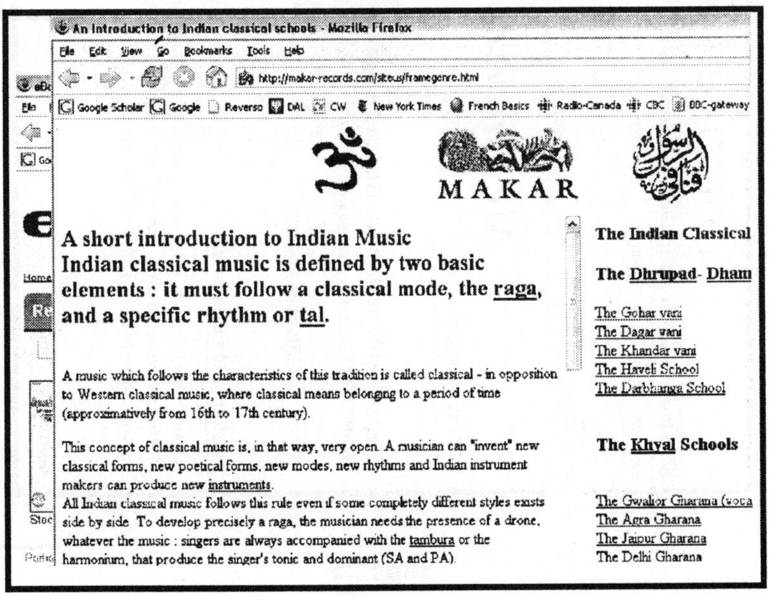

Slide 34

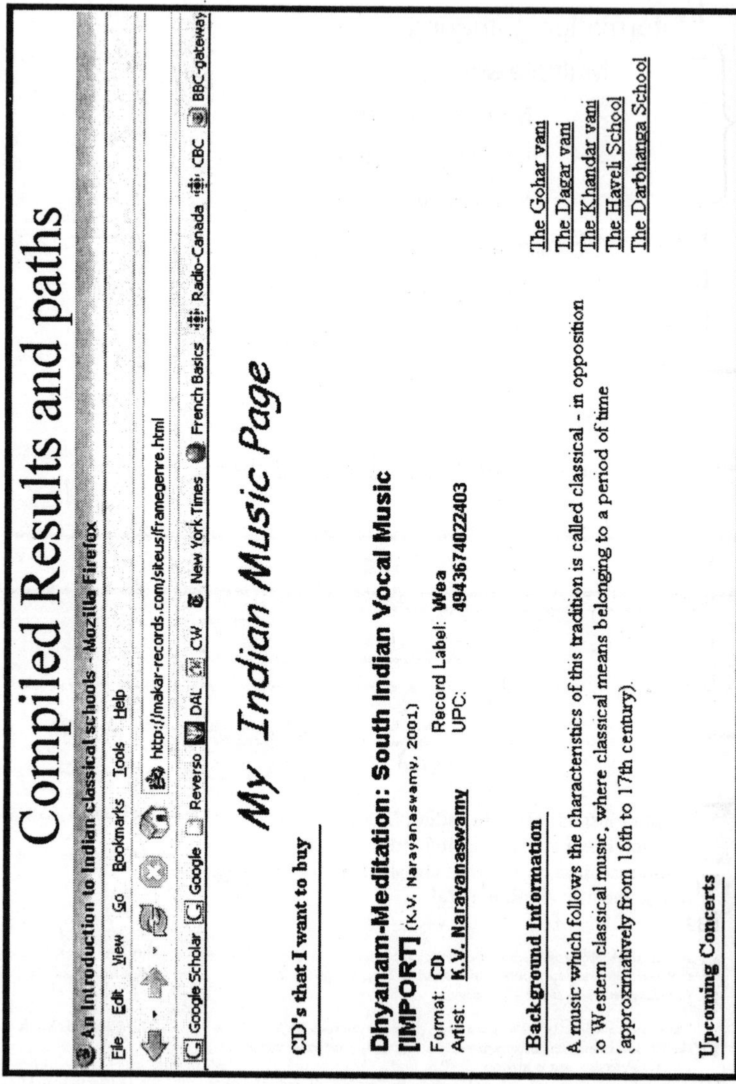
Compiled Results and paths
An Introduction to Indian classical schools - Mozilla Firefox
File Edit View Go Bookmarks Tools Help
http://makar-records.com/siteus/framegenre.html
Google Scholar Google Reverso DAL CW New York Times French Basics Radio-Canada CBC BBC-gateway
My Indian Music Page
CD's that I want to buy
Dhyanam-Meditation: South Indian Vocal Music [IMPORT] (K.V. Narayanaswamy, 2001)
Format: CD
Artist: K.V. Narayanaswamy
Record Label: Wea
UPC: 4943674022403
Background Information
A music which follows the characteristics of this tradition is called classical - in opposition to Western classical music, where classical means belonging to a period of time (approximatively from 16th to 17th century).
The Gohar vani
The Dagar vani
The Khandar vani
The Haveli School
The Darbhanga School
Upcoming Concerts

Slide 35

New Tools needed!

* If Information Gathering
  - Handle multiple pages
  - Bookmark sets of pages
  - Save/manage information within pages
  - Auto save URLs by session
* If FF -> easy cut & paste
* If transactions -> check if secure
* If new task – save current settings

Slide 36

Future Work

* What do we already know about supporting information seeking tasks in other contexts??
* Can we use this knowledge to design tools for browsers that support specific tasks?

Slide 37

Take home message

- The Web browser is now used for a wide range of tasks, most of which it was not designed to handle.
- Need to include task in the discussion of new features & in the evaluation of systems.
- *We either contort the task to fit the appliance or begin to redesign the appliance to support the tasks!*

Slide 38

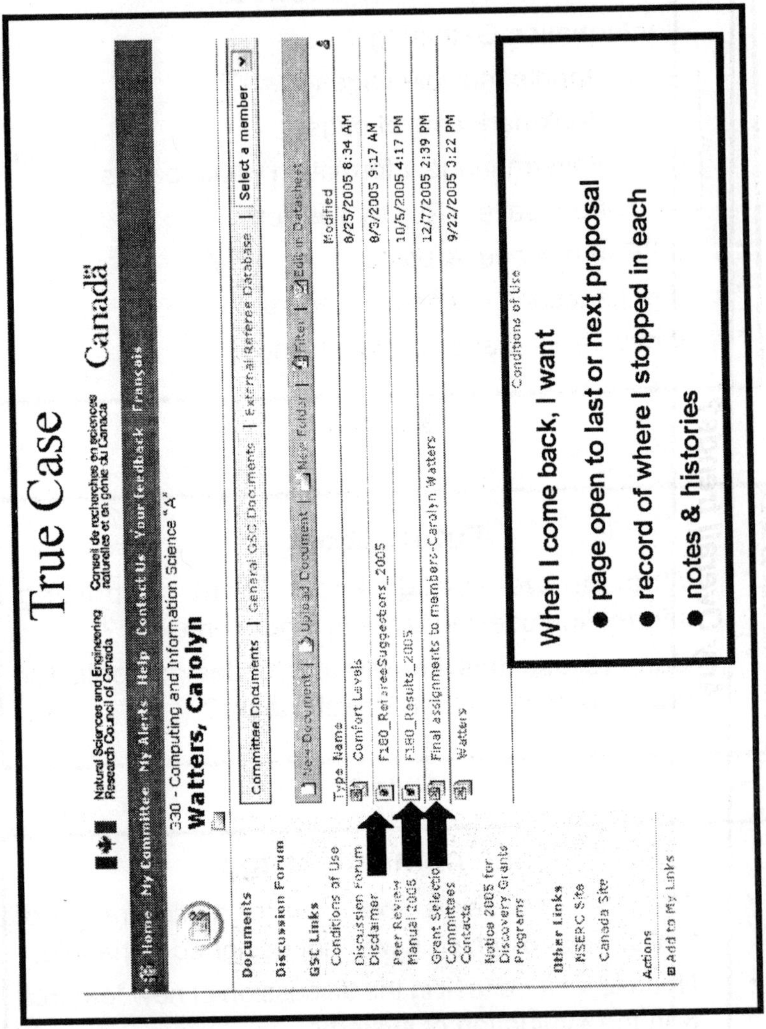
True Case
Watters, Carolyn
330 - Computing and Information Science "A"
When I come back, I want
● page open to last or next proposal
● record of where I stopped in each
● notes & histories

Slide 39

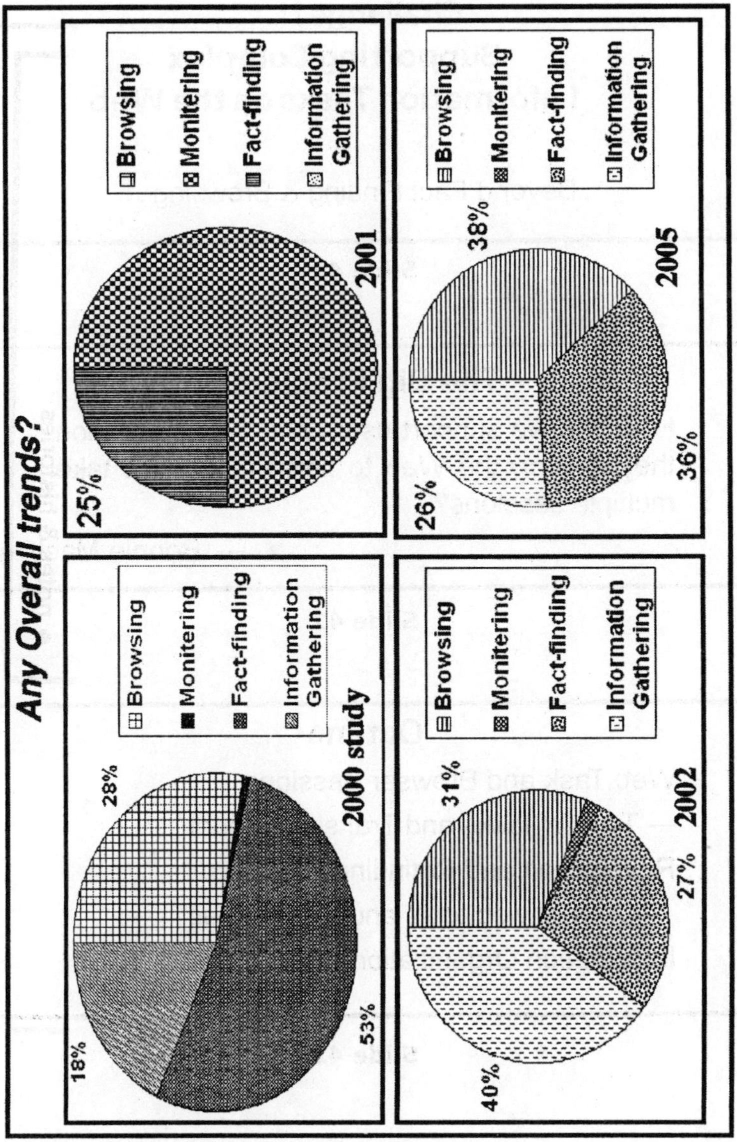
Any Overall trends?
18%
28%
53%
Browsing
Monitering
Fact-finding
Information Gathering
2000 study
25%
Browsing
Moniltering
Fact-finding
Information Gathering
2001
40%
27%
31%
Browsing
Monitering
Fact-finding
Information Gathering
2002
26%
36%
38%
Browsing
Monitering
Fact-finding
Information Gathering
2005

Slide 40

Challenge II.
Supporting Complex Information Tasks on the Web

Beyond Fact Finding & Browsing

Slide 41

The Big Problem

How can we support users *and* the information they find on the Web to finish tasks that take multiple sessions?

— Bonnie MacKay

Slide 42

Outline

* Web Task and Browser Sessions
  — Type of tasks and Transient Model
* Revisitation and Refinding Activities
  — Current web tools and approaches
* Information Organization

Slide 43

Problem

- * Shifting information needs from libraries and personal collections to the Web
- * No classification
- * No librarian
- * No quality control
- * One tool only: keyword search!!!

Slide 44

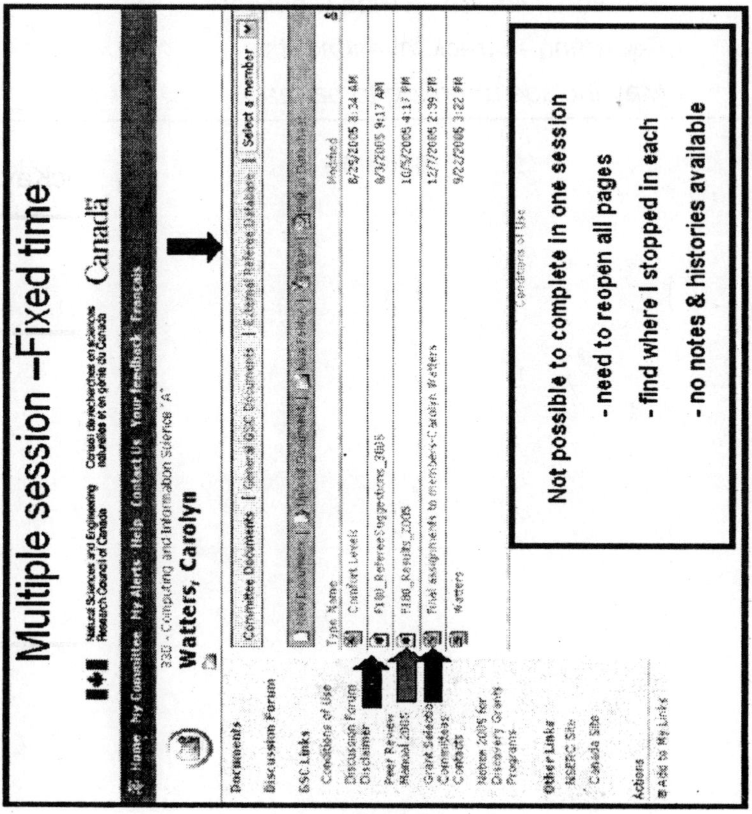

Slide 45

Notion of Session

* Single Session
  - Uninterrupted exclusive activity
  - Find a fact/ book a hotel
  - May include multiple pages
  - Avg. length 25 minutes
* Multi-Session
  - *Sequence of sessions related to same task*
  - *Time/goal limited -> Plan a holiday*
  - *Recurring -> track investments*
  - *May include returning to pages*

Slide 46

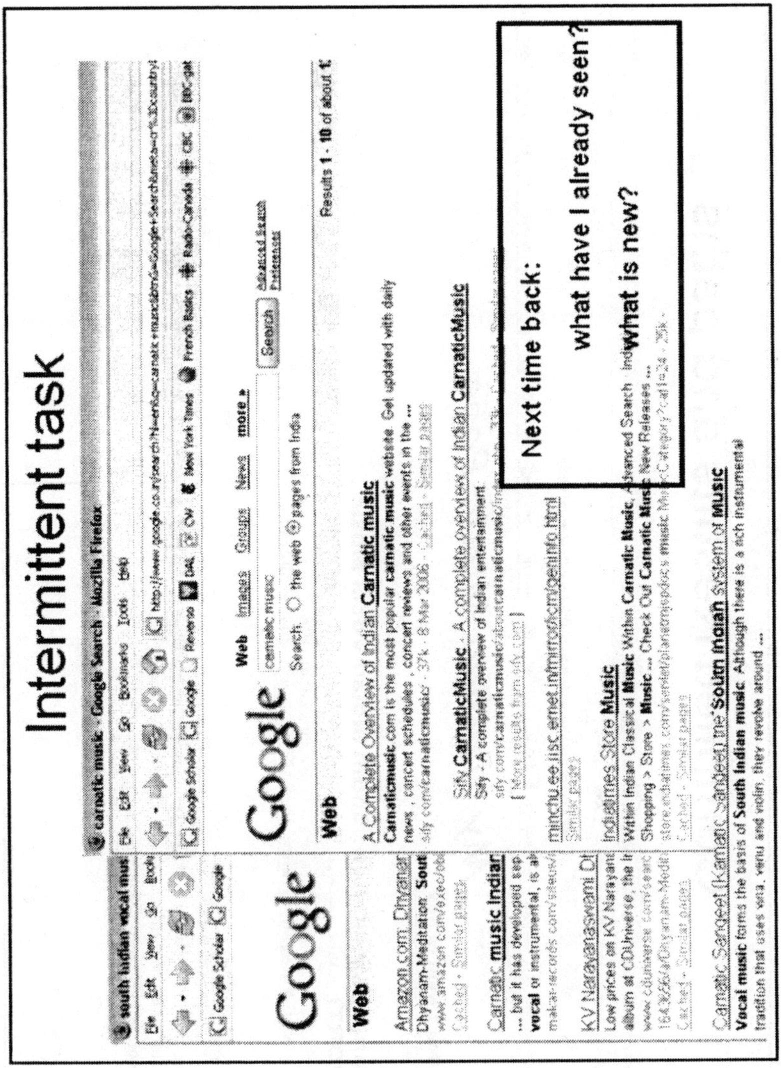
Intermittent task
Next time back:
what have I already seen?
what is new?

Slide 47

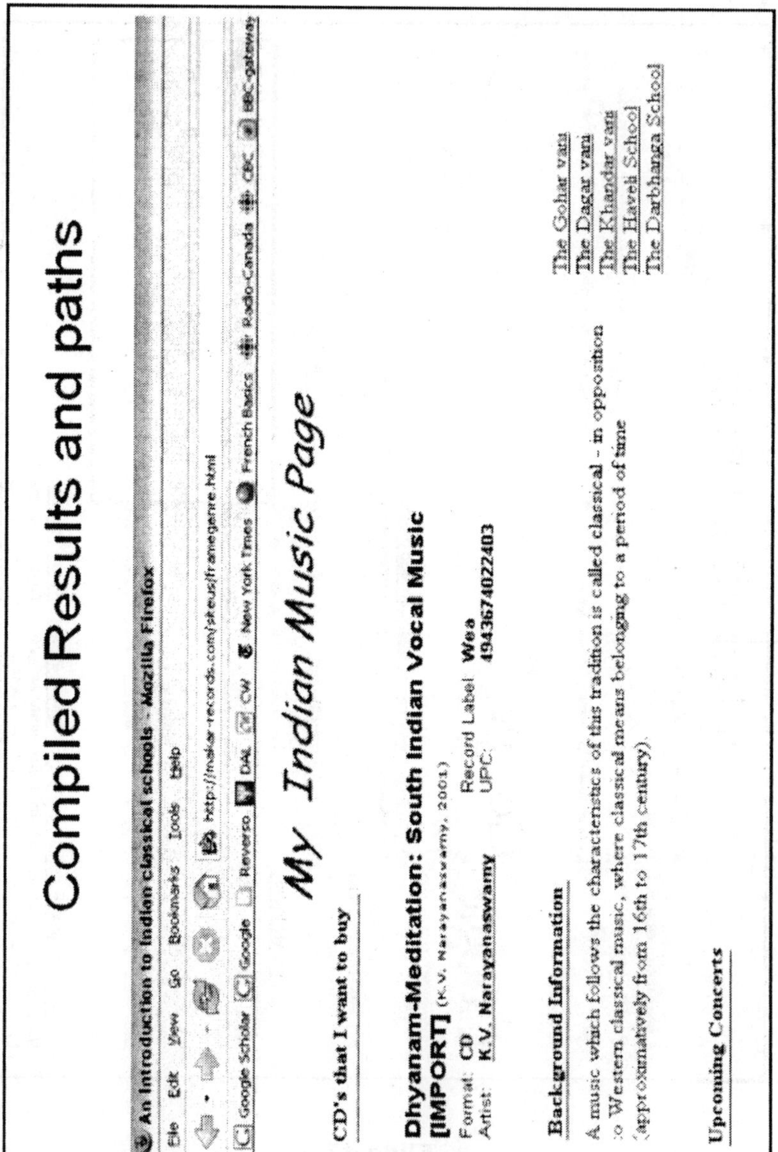
Compiled Results and paths
An Introduction to Indian classical schools - Mozilla Firefox
File Edit View Go Bookmarks Tools Help
My Indian Music Page
CD's that I want to buy
Dhyanam-Meditation: South Indian Vocal Music [IMPORT] (K.V. Narayanaswamy, 2001)
Format: CD
Artist: K.V. Narayanaswamy
Record Label: Wea
UPC: 1943674022403
Background Information
A music which follows the characteristics of this tradition is called classical - in opposition to Western classical music, where classical means belonging to a period of time (approximatively from 16th to 17th century).
The Gohar vani
The Dagar vani
The Khandar vani
The Haveli School
The Darbhanga School
Upcoming Concerts

Slide 48

Session and Tasks

* Single session (one time)
- Browsing
- Transactions
- Fact Finding

* Transient session (time/goal limited)
- Information gathering
- Accumulation of information

* Persistent session (recurring)
- Long term strategic use of information

Slide 49

Revisitation of Sources

* Web tasks often include revisiting
- Repetition of task
- Checking information to complete a task
- Monitoring

* Revisitation as a Common Activity
- 58% in a study by Tausher & Greenberg (1997)
- 81% in Cockburn study 2003
- 60% revisit once / 20% more than once

Slide 50

Web Tasks

Four Main Task Categories:

1. Fact Finding
2. Information Gathering
3. Browsing
4. Transactions

Slide 51

Revisitation and Refinding

* Two main revisiting tools on all browsers:

- History Lists
- Bookmarks (or Favorites)

Slide 52

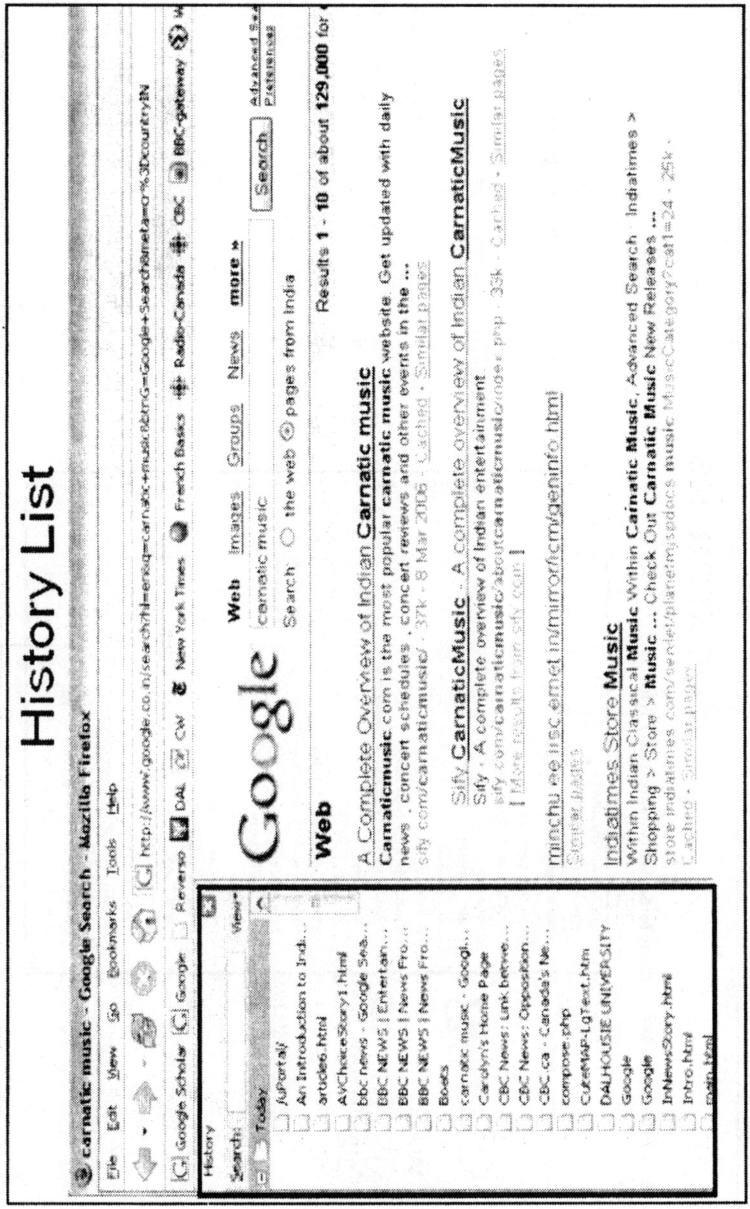
History List
carnatic music - Google Search - Mozilla Firefox
File Edit View Go Bookmarks Tools Help
Google
Web Images Groups News more »
Search
Results 1 - 10 of about 129,000 for
A Complete Overview of Indian Carnatic music
Sify CarnaticMusic - A complete overview of Indian CarnaticMusic
Indiatimes Store Music
History
Today

Slide 53

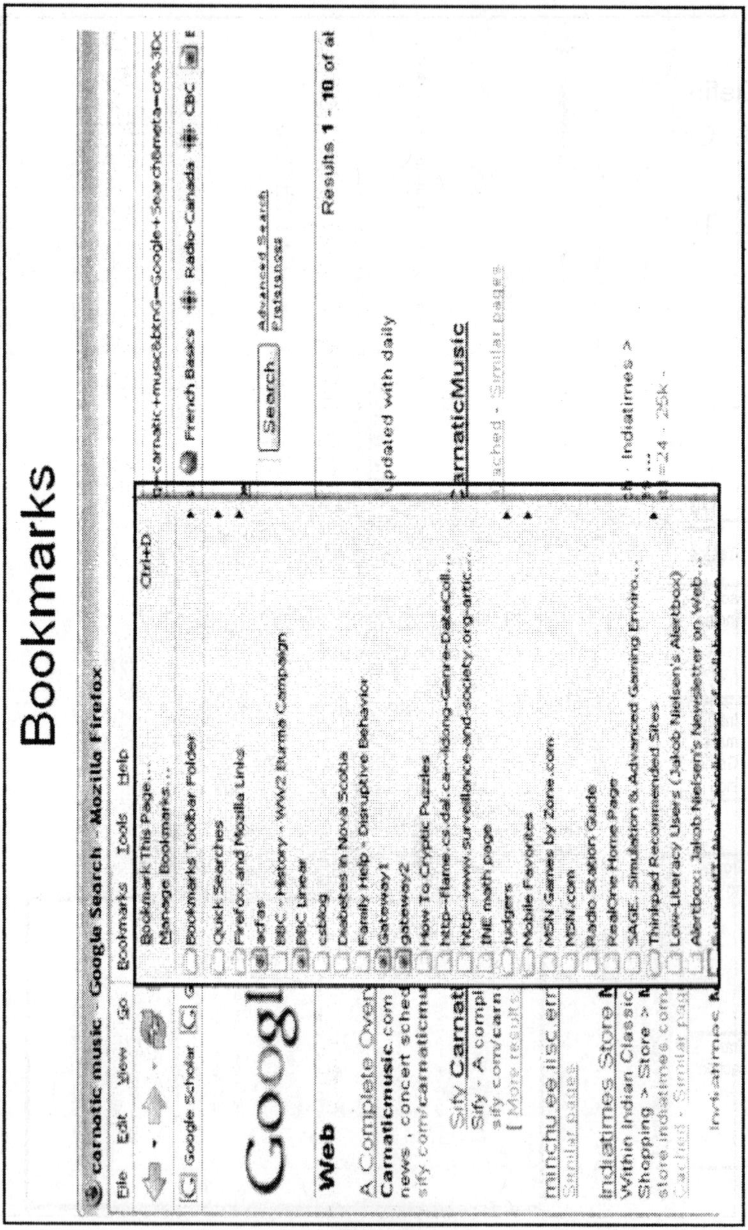
Bookmarks
carnatic music - Google Search - Mozilla Firefox
File Edit View Go Bookmarks Tools Help
Bookmark This Page... Ctrl+D
Manage Bookmarks...
Bookmarks Toolbar Folder
Quick Searches
Firefox and Mozilla Links
BBC - History - WW2 Blume Campaign
BBC Linear
Diabetes in Nova Scotia
Family Help - Disruptive Behavior
How To Cryptic Puzzles
MSN Games by Zone.com
MSN.com
Radio Station Guide
RealOne Home Page
Thinkpad Recommended Sites
Low-Literacy Users (Jakob Nielsen's Alertbox)
Search
Advanced Search
Results 1 - 10 of ab

Slide 54

Web Tasks

Defined by Two Features

1. Goal
   * The why or reason the task is being performed
2. Timeframe
   * Single Session (one time using browser)
   * Multiple Sessions (return to same information over more than one session)

Slide 55

Tasks	Goal Based	Type of Goals	Timeframe	Pages	Examples
Fact Finding	YES	Answer question, factual monitoring	Single session (monitoring for a set period or indefinite period still done during a single session each)	New and/ or seen	Find a restaurant to go to tonight, check the weather every day
Information Gathering	YES	Research comparison, decision making, support monitoring	Single session or several sessions, monitoring over set period or indefinite period	New and/ or seen	Examine a variety of factors to help decide which stock to buy, research paper, buy a new car
Browsing	NO	No specific goal, entertainment (ludic)	Single session (monitoring for a set period or indefinite period seen still done during a single session each)	New and/ or seen	Following a link for interest, read the entertainment section, look at ebay with no particular item in mind to buy
Transaction	YES	Communication, provide and request information, action based	Single session, (monitoring for New and/or a set period or indefinite period seen still done during a single session each)	New and/ or seen	Email, banking, filling in a form

Slide 56

Browser Sessions

Browser Session Types

Single Session

Multiple Sessions

- **Transient** (definable goal and timeframe)
- **Persistent** (less definable goal and timeframe)

Slide 57

Single Session

- **Tasks**
  - Fact Finding
  - Browsing
  - Transactions
  - Information gathering
- **Goals**
  - specific goal
  - no specific goal
  - specific action
  - specific & nonspecific
- Revisitation also occurs in single sessions
  - Repeat action e.g. read the news
  - Review action e.g. back up to previous page

Slide 58

Transient Sessions

* Information gathering
  - Larger in scope
  - Time & Goal frame expanded
  - Multiple dimensions (flight & hotel, etc)
* Goal
  - Not well defined (report on, find out about)
* Revisitation
  - Updating /revising
  - Completing

Slide 59

Transient Session Scenario

* Collecting background material for research project on genre
* 3 week duration
* Goals
  – Analysis and synthesis of current work
  – List of citations

Slide 60

Persistent Sessions

* No time constraint
* Long range interest
* Monitor for new information
* *Information Retrieval*
* *Asthma in Children*
* *South Indian Vocal Music*

Slide 61

Persistent Session Scenario

* Interest in Information Retrieval
* Duration is indefinite
* Goals
  — Identify new trends
    * Folksonomies
    * blogs
  — Monitor known sites
    * ACM digital library
  — Aggregate sources and citations
    * Add links
    * Read papers
    * Create a report or a web site

Slide 62

Browser Sessions
Transient Model

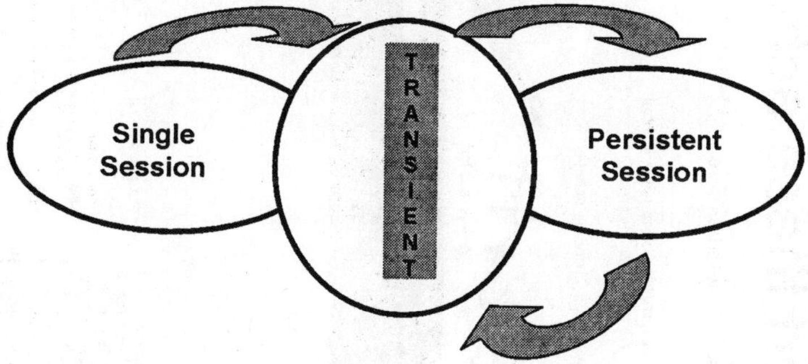

Slide 63

Context

* We make the following assumptions:
  - Information gathering and monitoring tasks involve revisitation to the same web pages & web sites
  - Users may spontaneously morph between session types

Slide 64

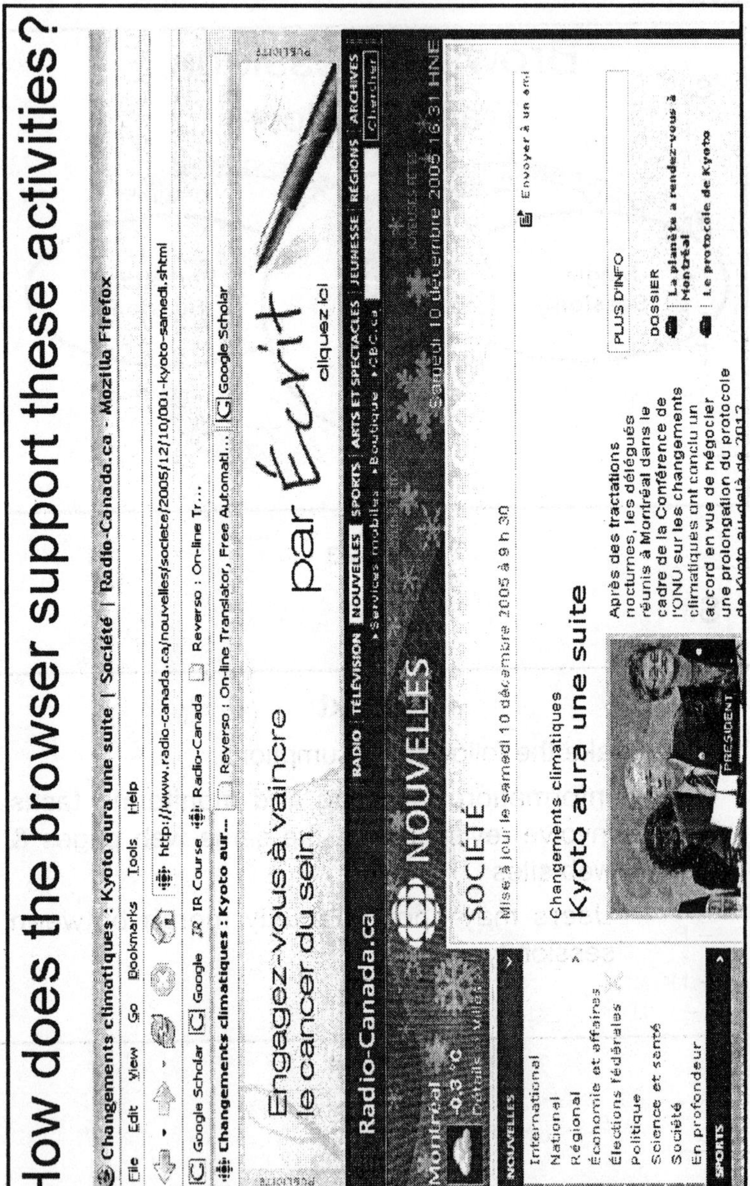
How does the browser support these activities?
Changements climatiques : Kyoto aura une suite | Société | Radio-Canada.ca - Mozilla Firefox
File Edit View Go Bookmarks Tools Help
http://www.radio-canada.ca/nouvelles/societe/2005/12/10/001-kyoto-samedi.shtml
Google Scholar Google IR Course Radio-Canada Reverso : On-line Tr...
Radio-Canada.ca
NOUVELLES
SOCIÉTÉ
Changements climatiques
Kyoto aura une suite
Engagez-vous à vaincre le cancer du sein
par Écrit
cliquez ici
International
National
Régional
Économie et affaires
Élections fédérales
Politique
Science et santé
Société
En profondeur
PLUS D'INFO
DOSSIER
La planète a rendez-vous à Montréal
Le protocole de Kyoto

Slide 65

Support Needed by Users

* Single Sessions

- Fact finding
- Browsing

* Transient Sessions

- Saving results
- Resuming task

* Persistent Sessions

- **Restarting

Slide 66

Simple task/single session Fact Finding

- Fact Finding
  - Articulation of search
  - Selection of most likely source
  - Read
  - Select fact
- Support
  - Search bar
  - Bookmarks
  - Hit list

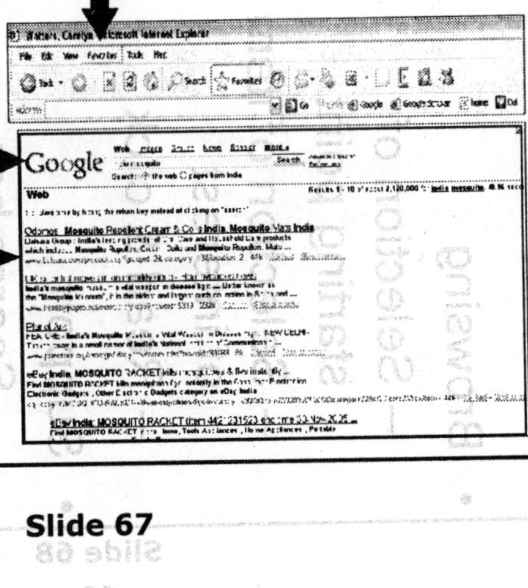

Slide 67

Browsing

- Browsing
  - Selection of starting point
  - Selection of item of interest
  - Read & click
- Support
  - Search bar
  - Type URL
  - Hit list
  - Hyperlinks

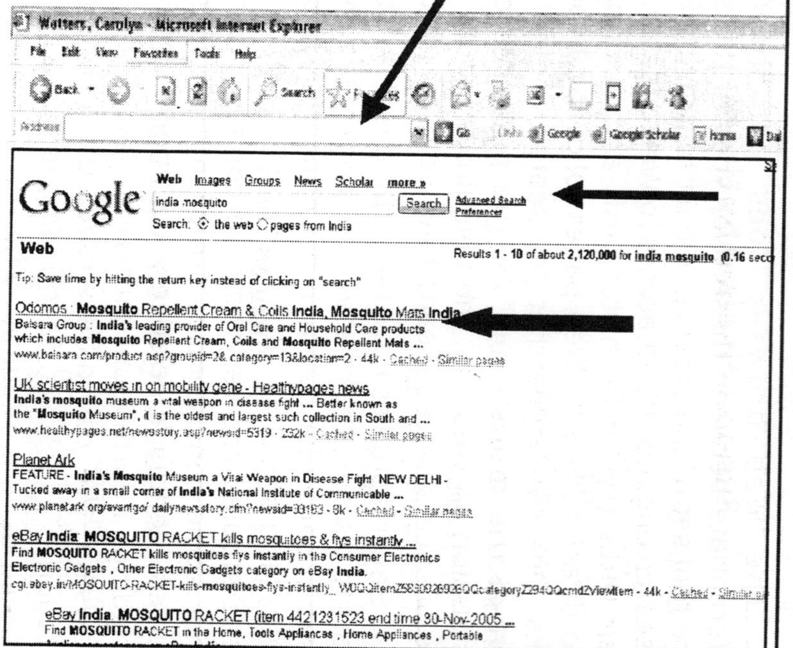

Transient Sessions

* Complex tasks
  - May be interrupted
  - May be intermittent
  - May be sequence of actions

Information gathering

Slide 69

Complex Task Example

* Grant review panel
* Time period 3 weeks
* Goal – prepare reviews for 50 proposals
* Information per proposal
  - List of potential reviewers
  - Application forms
  - Applicant cvs
  - Review forms
* Interface – Web browser!

Slide 70

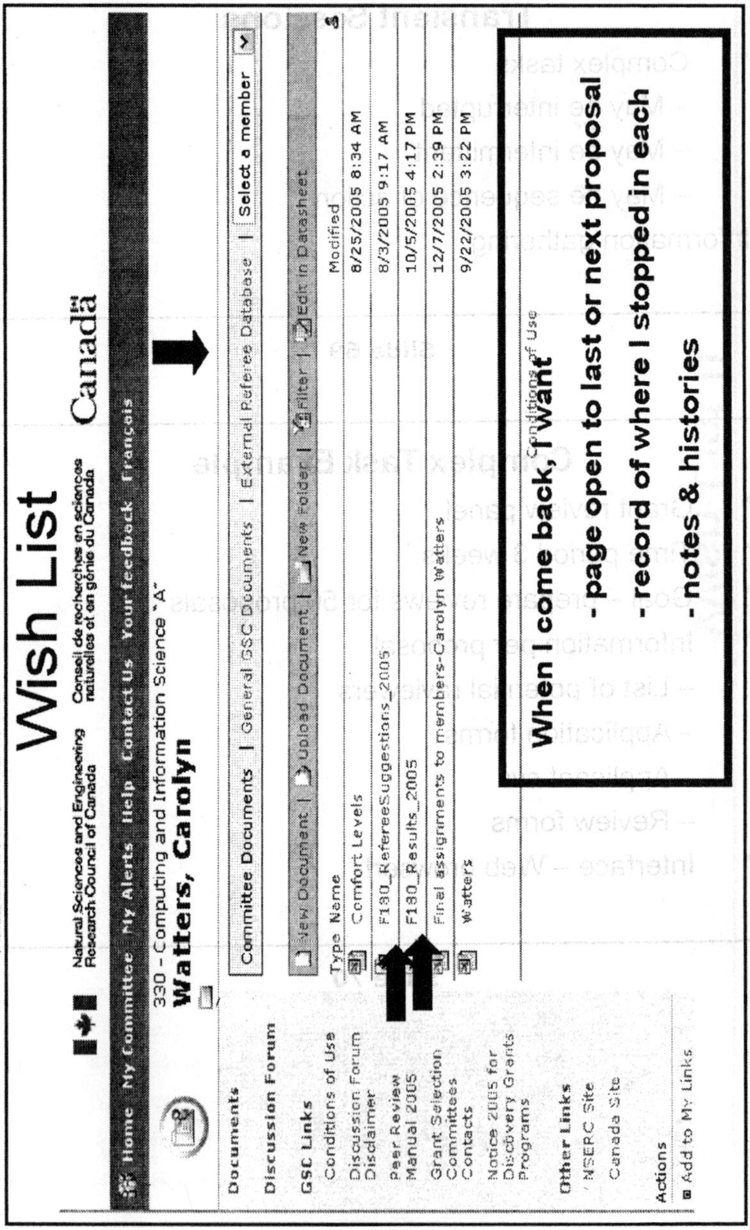
Wish List
Natural Sciences and Engineering Research Council of Canada
Conseil de recherches en sciences naturelles et en génie du Canada
Canada
Home My Committee My Alerts Help Contact Us Your feedback Français
330 - Computing and Information Science "A"
Watters, Carolyn
Documents
Discussion Forum
GSC Links
Conditions of Use
Discussion Forum Disclaimer
Peer Review Manual 2005
Grant Selection Committees Contacts
Notice 2005 for Discovery Grants Programs
Other Links
NSERC Site
Canada Site
Actions
Add to My Links
Committee Documents | General GSC Documents | External Referee Database | Select a member
New Document | Upload Document | New Folder | Filter | Edit in Datasheet
Type Name Modified
Comfort Levels 8/25/2005 8:34 AM
F180_RefereeSuggestions_2005 8/3/2005 9:17 AM
F180_Results_2005 10/5/2005 4:17 PM
Final assignments to members-Carolyn Watters 12/7/2005 2:39 PM
Watters 9/22/2005 3:22 PM
Conditions of Use
When I come back, I want
- page open to last or next proposal
- record of where I stopped in each
- notes & histories

Slide 71

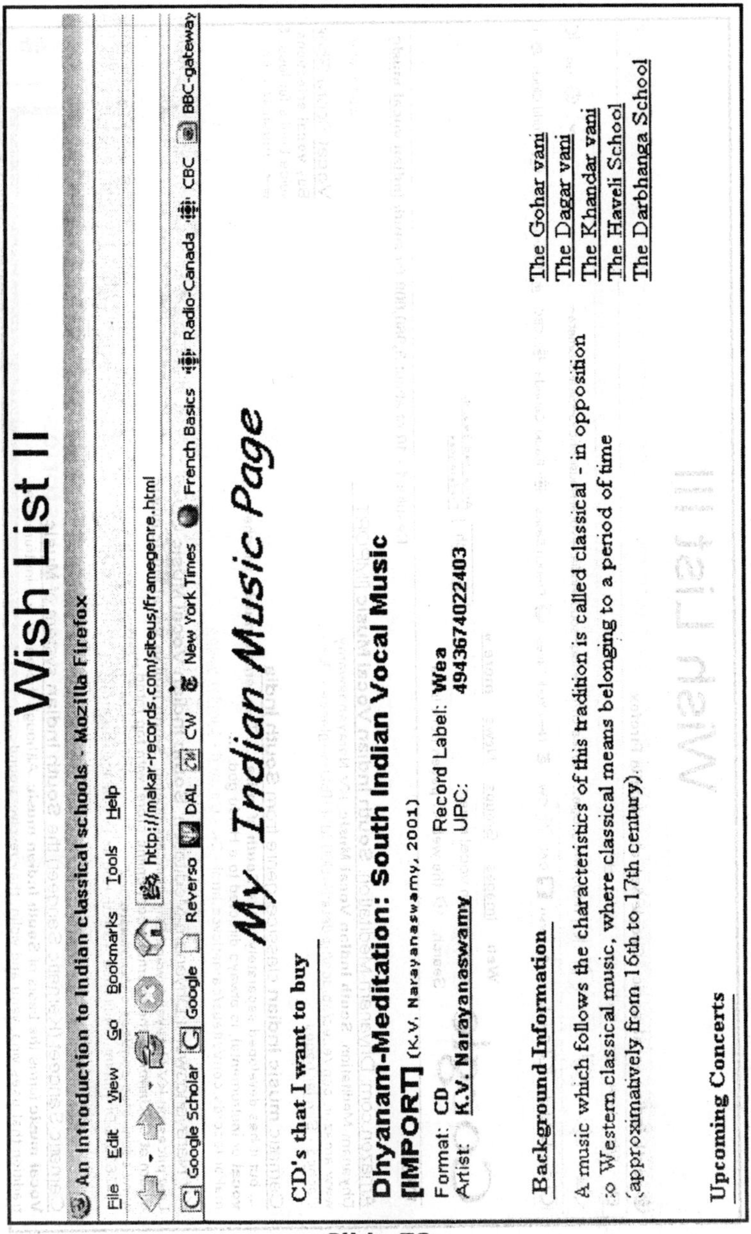
Wish List II
An Introduction to Indian classical schools - Mozilla Firefox
File Edit View Go Bookmarks Tools Help
http://makar-records.com/siteus/framegenre.html
Google Scholar Google Reverso DAL CW New York Times French Basics Radio-Canada CBC BBC-gateway
My Indian Music Page
CD's that I want to buy
Dhyanam-Meditation: South Indian Vocal Music [IMPORT] (K.V. Narayanaswamy, 2001)
Format: CD
Artist: K.V. Narayanaswamy
Record Label: Wea
UPC: 4943674022403
Background Information
A music which follows the characteristics of this tradition is called classical - in opposition to Western classical music, where classical means belonging to a period of time (approximatively from 16th to 17th century).
The Gohar vani
The Dagar vani
The Khandar vani
The Haveli School
The Darbhanga School
Upcoming Concerts

Slide 72

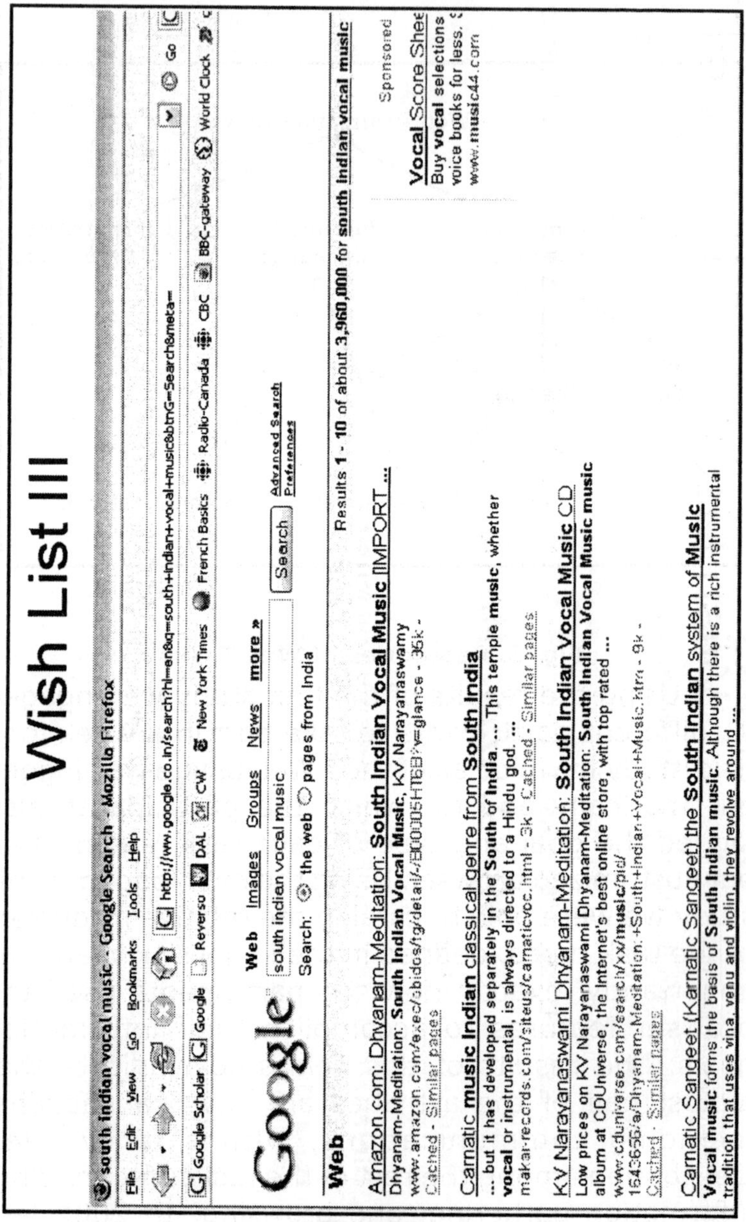
Wish List III
south indian vocal music - Google Search - Mozilla Firefox
File Edit View Go Bookmarks Tools Help
http://ww.google.co.in/search?hl=en&q=south+indian+vocal+music&btnG=Search&meta=
Google Scholar Google Reverso DAL CW New York Times French Basics Radio-Canada CBC BBC-gateway World Clock
Google
Web Images Groups News more »
south indian vocal music
Search
Advanced Search
Preferences
Search: the web pages from India
Web
Results 1 - 10 of about 3,960,000 for south indian vocal music
Amazon.com: Dhyanam-Meditation: South Indian Vocal Music [IMPORT ...
Dhyanam-Meditation: South Indian Vocal Music, KV Narayanaswamy
www.amazon.com/exec/obidos/tg/detail/-/B00005HT6B?v=glance - 35k -
Cached - Similar pages
Carnatic music Indian classical genre from South India
... but it has developed separately in the South of India. ... This temple music, whether vocal or instrumental, is always directed to a Hindu god. ...
makar-records.com/siteus/carnaticvoc.html - 3k - Cached - Similar pages
KV Narayanaswami Dhyanam-Meditation: South Indian Vocal Music CD
Low prices on KV Narayanaswami Dhyanam-Meditation: South Indian Vocal Music music album at CDUniverse, the Internet's best online store, with top rated ...
www.cduniverse.com/search/xx/music/pid/1643656/a/Dhyanam-Meditation:+South+Indian+Vocal+Music.htm - 9k -
Cached - Similar pages
Carnatic Sangeet (Karnatic Sangeet) the South Indian system of Music
Vocal music forms the basis of South Indian music. Although there is a rich instrumental tradition that uses vina, venu and violin, they revolve around ...
Sponsored
www.music44.com

Slide 73

Current Support for Transient Sessions

* Favorites/bookmarks
* Tabs

Slide 74

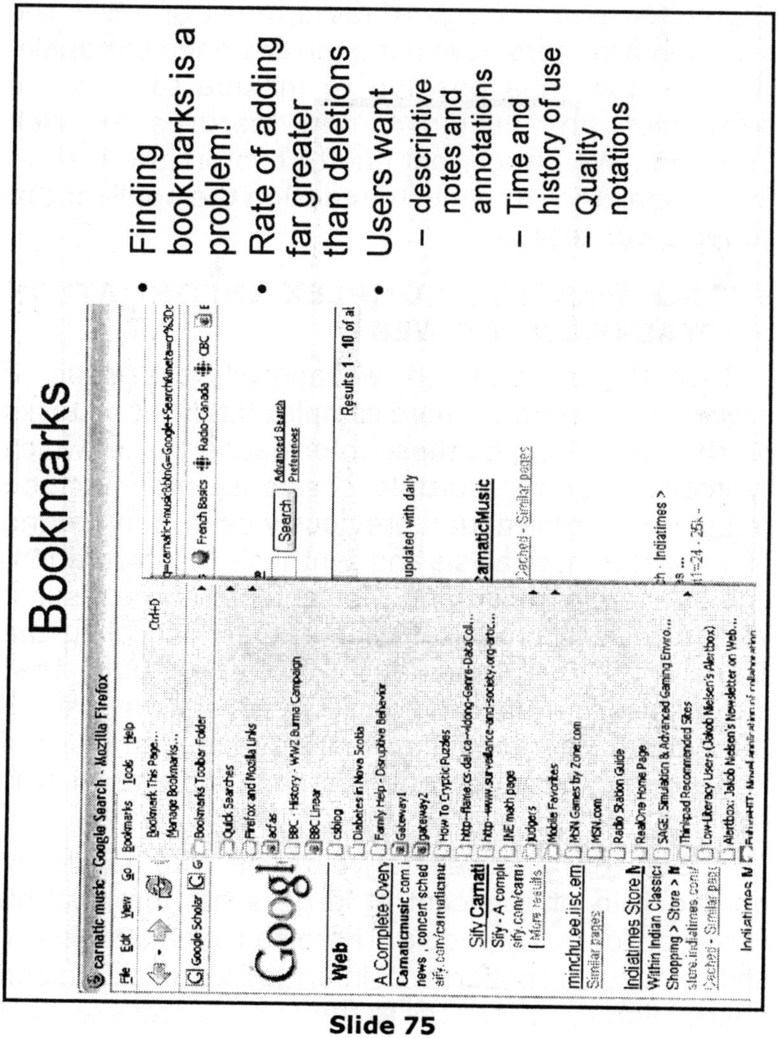

Slide 75

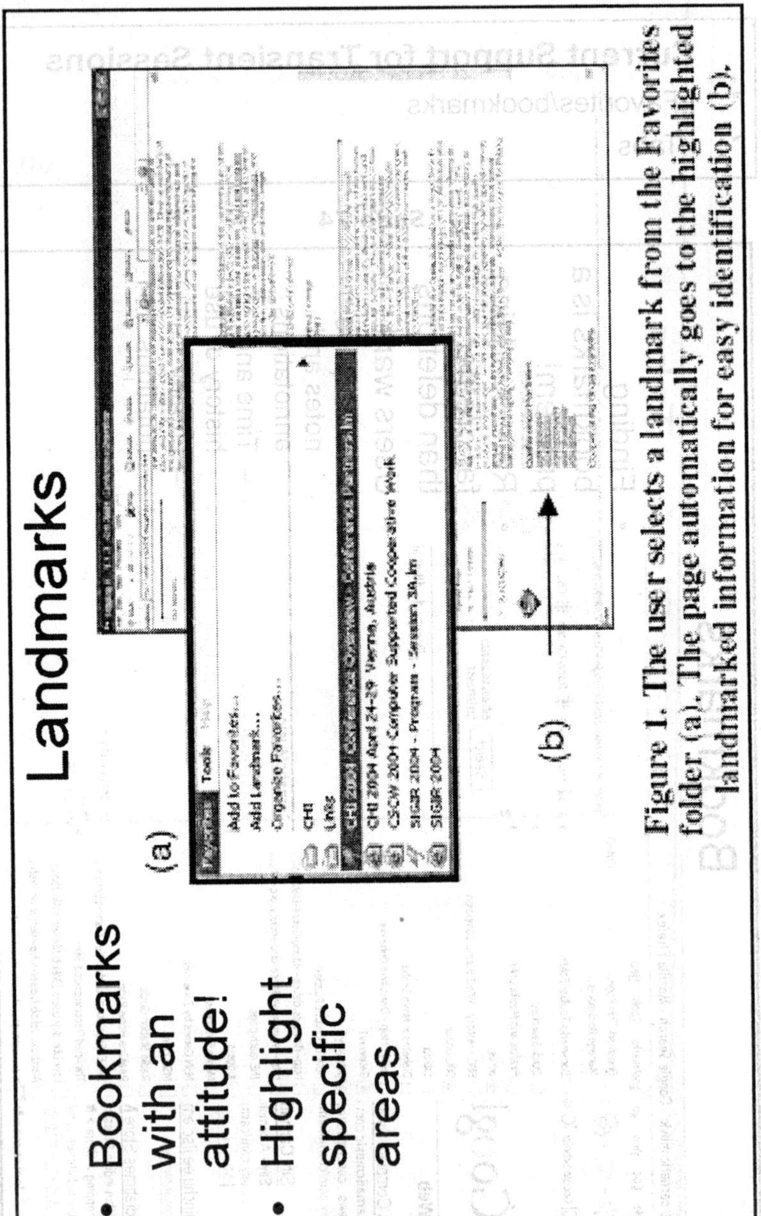
Landmarks
• Bookmarks with an attitude!
• Highlight specific areas
(a)
Favorites
Tools
Add to Favorites...
Add Landmark...
Organize Favorites...
CHI
Links
CHI 2004 April 24-29 Vienna, Austria
CSCW 2004 Computer Supported Cooperative Work
SIGIR 2004
(b)
Figure 1. The user selects a landmark from the Favorites folder (a). The page automatically goes to the highlighted landmarked information for easy identification (b).

Slide 76

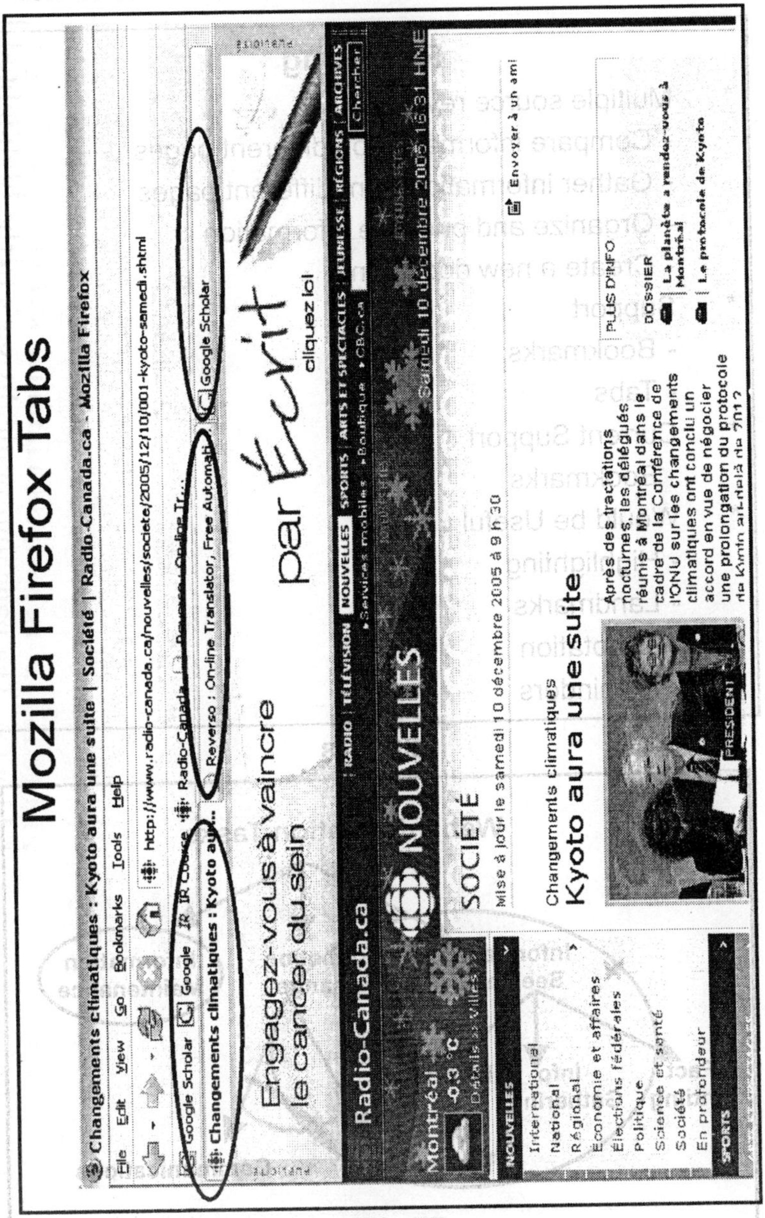
Mozilla Firefox Tabs
Changements climatiques : Kyoto aura une suite | Société | Radio-Canada.ca - Mozilla Firefox
File Edit View Go Bookmarks Tools Help
http://www.radio-canada.ca/nouvelles/societe/2005/12/10/001-kyoto-samedi.shtml
Changements climatiques : Kyoto au...
Reverso : On-line Translator, Free Automati
Google Scholar
Engagez-vous à vaincre le cancer du sein
par Écrit
cliquez ici
Radio-Canada.ca
NOUVELLES
SOCIÉTÉ
Mise à jour le samedi 10 décembre 2005 à 9 h 30
Changements climatiques
Kyoto aura une suite

Slide 77

Revisiting

* Multiple source revisiting
  - Compare information on different pages
  - Gather information from different pages
  - Organize and prioritize information
  - Create a new document
* Support
  - Bookmarks
  - Tabs
* Current Support
  - Bookmarks
* Would be Useful
  - Highlighting
  - Landmarks
  - Annotation
  - Reminders

Slide 78

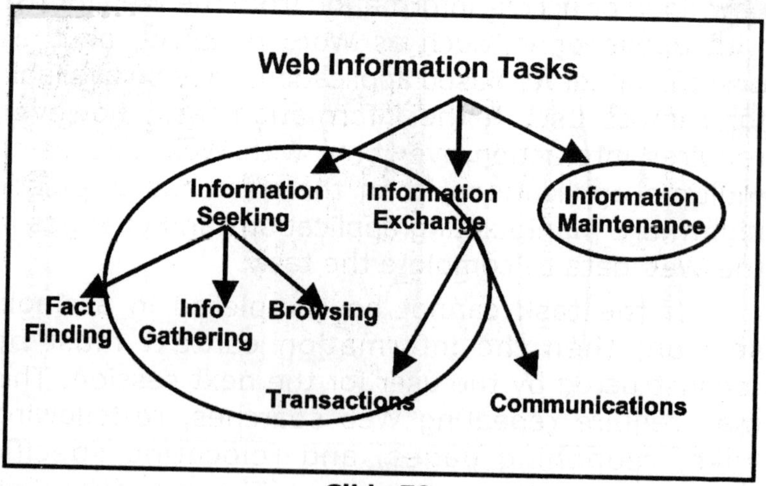

Slide 79

PIMs

- Personal Information Management tools
- How do we manage the information we gather?

Slide 80

Information Organization

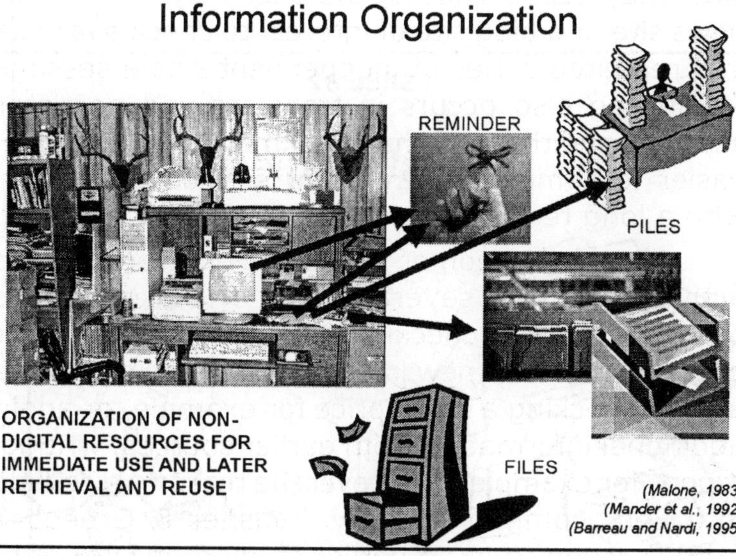

Slide 81

Users & Information Organization

* Web users multitask (Spink et al, 2004)
* Users avoid complex filing schemes
* 3 types of information
  - – Short shelf life (memo)
  - – In progress (report)
  - – Archival (research interest)
* Integrate web information with other information storage schemes

Slide 82

PIM strategies

Copyright 2004 by Randy Glasbergen.
www.glasbergen.com

"I am not disorganized — I know *exactly* where everything is! The newer stuff is on top and the older stuff is on the bottom."

Slide 83

Personal Information Organization

- Digital examples:
  - pilers (all messages in one box)
  - and filers (messages into file folders) *(Whittaker and Sidner, 1996)*
  - Stuff I've Seen (SIS) *(Dumais et al., 2003)*

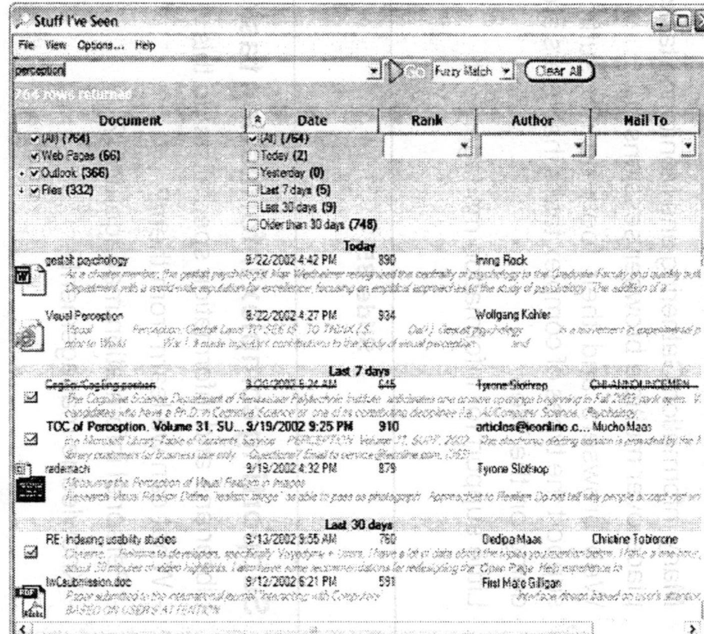

Slide 84

The Problem

* Many Information Gathering and Monitoring tasks take place over multiple browser sessions
* Web browsers and their tools do not sufficiently support the types of complex tasks that users are now doing on the Web
* Little support for information management

Slide 85

Supporting complex information tasks

* Librarians and information specialists do this
  - What can we learn from them?
  - Personal information management?
  - Knowledge management?

Slide 86

Open Questions

* Should we move Web searching out from the browser into the applications (Word, excel, etc)?
* Can we detect shifts in user goals?
* What are the essential functions of the next generation of Web appliances??

Slide 87

Challenge III:

How to categorize Web Search results to support tasks?

Slide 88

Problem

* Search engines provide access to pages which satisfy the search query but not the user expectation
* How can we help the user focus on the search results

Slide 89

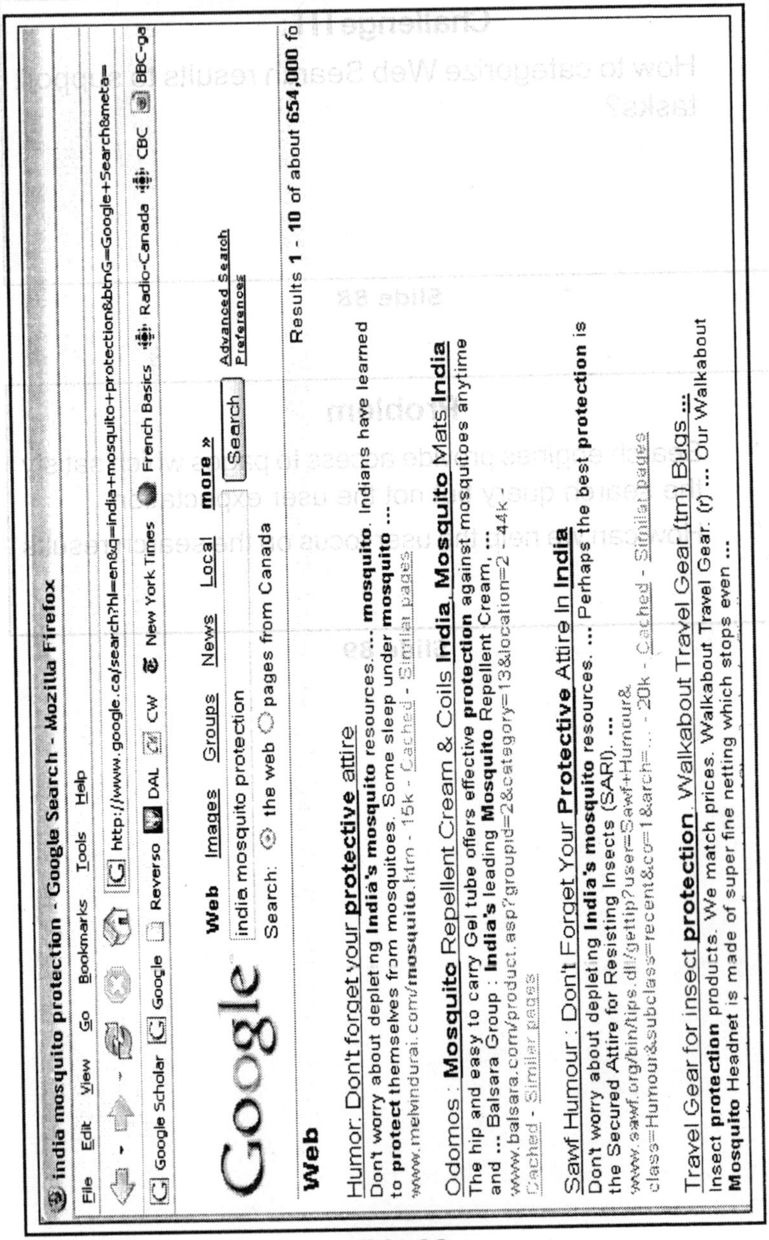
india mosquito protection - Google Search - Mozilla Firefox
File Edit View Go Bookmarks Tools Help
http://www.google.ca/search?hl=en&q=india+mosquito+protection&btnG=Google+Search&meta=
Google Scholar Google Reverso DAL CW New York Times French Basics Radio-Canada CBC BBC-ga
Google
Web Images Groups News Local more »
india mosquito protection
Search
Advanced Search
Preferences
Search: the web pages from Canada
Web
Results 1 - 10 of about 654,000 fo
Humor: Don't forget your protective attire
Don't worry about depleting India's mosquito resources. ... mosquito. Indians have learned to protect themselves from mosquitoes. Some sleep under mosquito ...
www.melvindurai.com/mosquito.htm - 15k - Cached - Similar pages
Odomos : Mosquito Repellent Cream & Coils India, Mosquito Mats India
The hip and easy to carry Gel tube offers effective protection against mosquitoes anytime and ... Balsara Group : India's leading Mosquito Repellent Cream, ...
www.balsara.com/product.asp?groupid=2&category=13&location=2 - 44k -
Cached - Similar pages
Sawf Humour : Don't Forget Your Protective Attire In India
Don't worry about depleting India's mosquito resources. ... Perhaps the best protection is the Secured Attire for Resisting Insects (SARI). ...
www.sawf.org/bin/tips.dll/gettip?user=Sawf+Humour&class=Humour&subclass=recent&co=1&arch=... - 20k - Cached - Similar pages
Travel Gear for insect protection. Walkabout Travel Gear(tm) Bugs ...
Insect protection products. We match prices. Walkabout Travel Gear. (r) ... Our Walkabout Mosquito Headnet is made of super fine netting which stops even ...

Slide 90

Web Information Resources

* Why? (task)
  - Find, Compare/Choose, Understand
* What? (content)
  - Business, Education, Finance, Job Search, Medical, Miscellaneous News, People, Produce Info & Purchase and Travel
* Form ?? (genre)

Slide 91

Genre and Information Seeking

* What is genre
* Relationship to user task
* Evolution of genre
* Classification of Genre
* Detection of Genre

M.Shepherd, J.Duffy & L.Dong, R. Zhang

Slide 92

Genre

* "Classifying statement"
* Form + content
  - Newspaper
  - Mystery novel
* Rhetorical style (Miller, 1984)
  - Essay, poem, novel
* Socially recognized communicative purposes (Orlikowski, 1994)
  - Office memo, income statement

Slide 93

Digital Genre

* Orlikowski & Yates (1994)
  - "A distinctive type of communicative action, characterized by a socially recognized communicative purpose and common aspects of form"
  - Communication focus
  - Social construct
  - Purpose + <form, content>

Slide 94

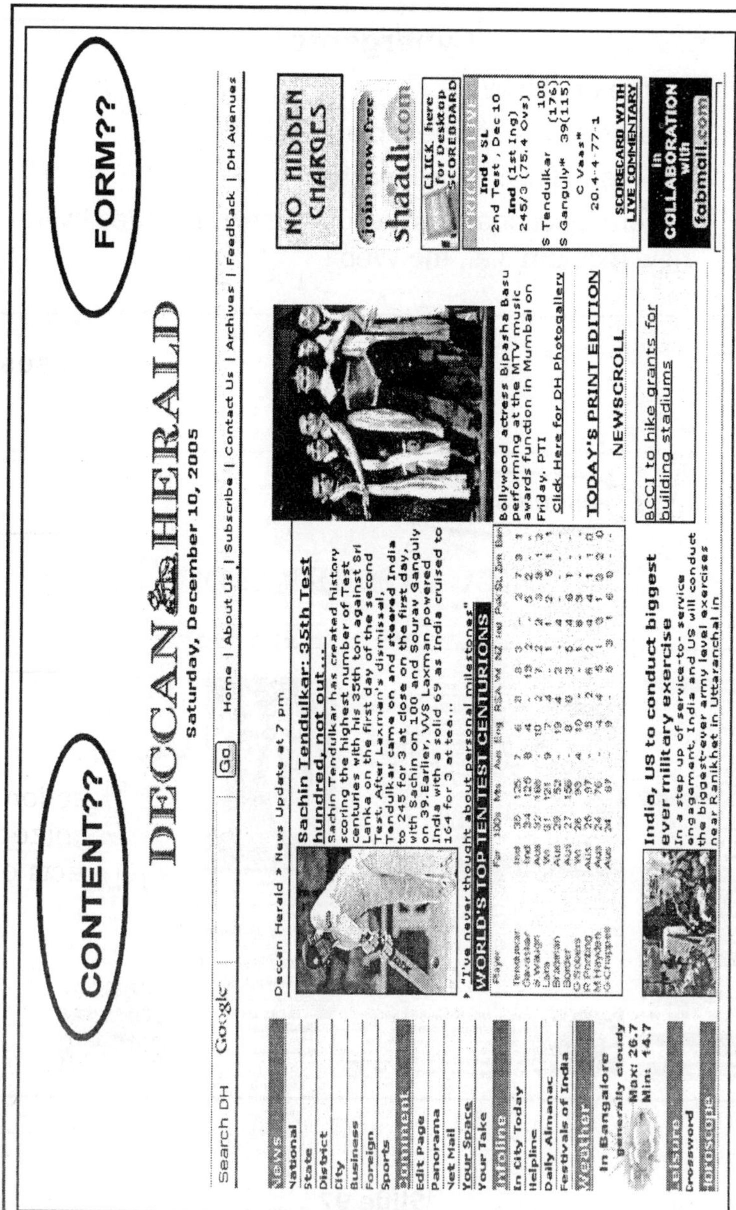
CONTENT??
FORM??
DECCAN HERALD
Saturday, December 10, 2005
Search DH
Go
Home | About Us | Subscribe | Contact Us | Archives | Feedback | DH Avenues
Deccan Herald » News Update at 7 pm
Sachin Tendulkar: 35th Test hundred, not out...
"I've never thought about personal milestones"
WORLD'S TOP TEN TEST CENTURIONS
India, US to conduct biggest ever military exercise
Bollywood actress Bipasha Basu performing at the MTV music awards function in Mumbai on Friday. PTI
Click Here for DH Photogallery
TODAY'S PRINT EDITION
NEWSCROLL
BCCI to hike grants for building stadiums
NO HIDDEN CHARGES
Join now. free
shaadi.com
Ind v SL
2nd Test, Dec 10
SCORECARD WITH LIVE COMMENTARY
In COLLABORATION with fabmall.com
News
National
State
District
City
Business
Foreign
Sports
Comment
Edit Page
Panorama
Net Mail
Your Space
Your Take
Infoline
In City Today
Helpline
Daily Almanac
Festivals of India
Weather
In Bangalore
generally cloudy
Max: 26.7
Min: 14.7
Leisure
Crossword
Horoscope

Slide 95

Cybergenre

- * Genre on the Web
- * Characterized by the tuple
  <content, form, functionality>
- * Where functionality is the functionality afforded by the new medium, i.e., the Web

Slide 96

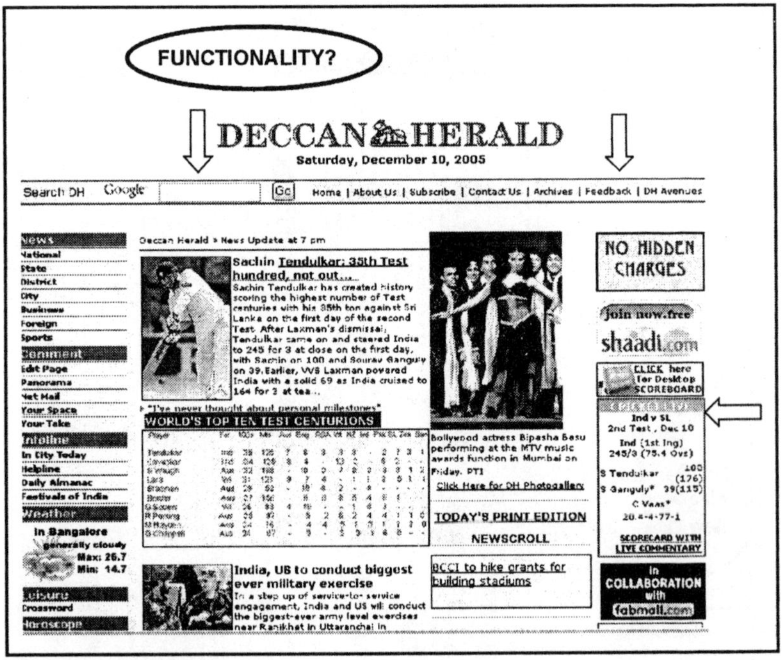

Slide 97

Evolution of CyberGenre

* 10 billion web documents
* Genre on the Web
  - Journal Paper genre
  - Film/video genre
  - Catalog genre
  - Home Page genre
  - .....
* Rapid evolution

Slide 98

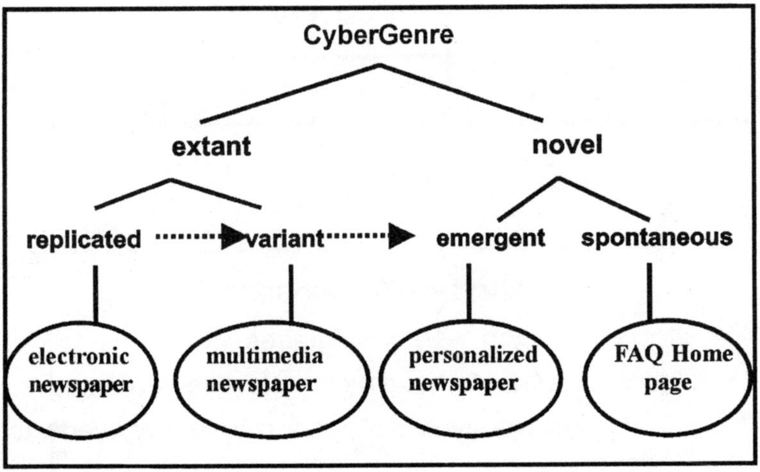

Slide 99

Categories of Web Genre				
Genre	**Purpose**	**Content**	**Form**	**Functionality**
home page	introduction	about owner	text/image/ links	links, email
article	topical information	text	structure author	links, search
catalog	listing	list of prods & services	list, tables images	purchase search, link
discussion	opinions	responses	threaded lists, blogs.	respond search
news	current awareness	news items images	broadsheet short items	search, link
FAQ	help	Q & As	list of Q&A	search
dictionary	definitions	term definitions	alphabetic list	scroll, link
entertainment	entertain	games videos	multimedia	interactive download

Slide 100

Motivation for Research

* Google indexed > 10 billion pages
* Problem is how to have more selective searching
* Classifying retrieved web pages by genre leads to better precision

Slide 101

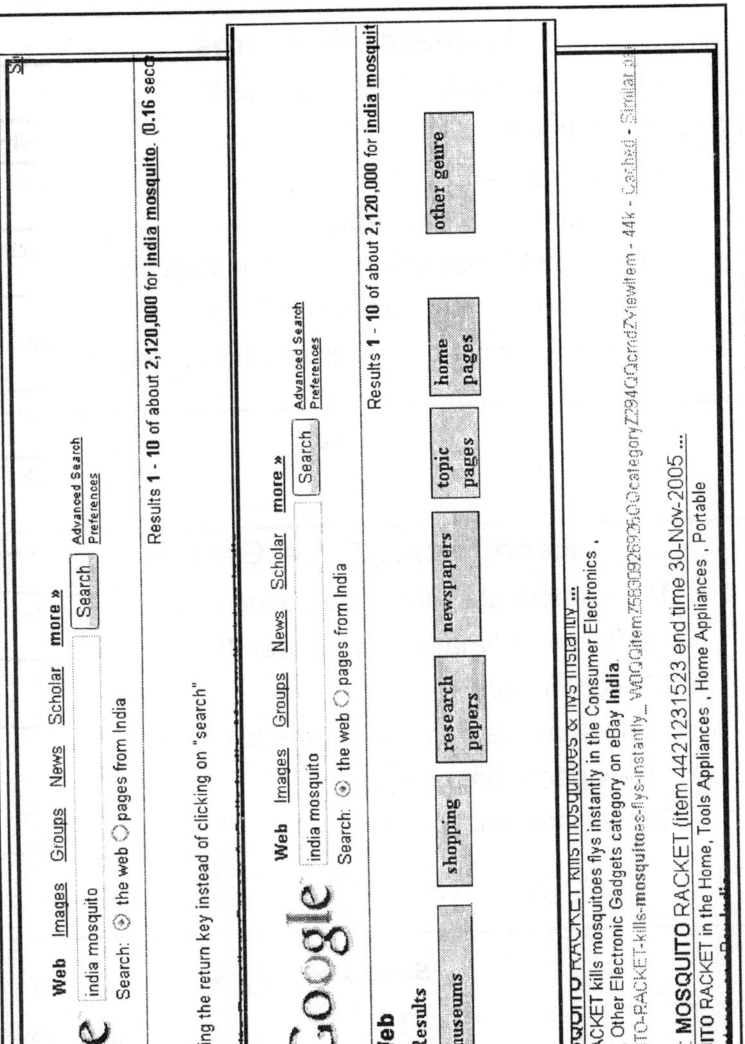
Google
Web Images Groups News Scholar more »
india mosquito
Search
Advanced Search
Preferences
Search: the web pages from India
Web
Results 1 - 10 of about 2,120,000 for india mosquito
Results
museums
shopping
research papers
newspapers
topic pages
home pages
other genre
Tip: Save time by hitting the return key instead of clicking on "search"
Planet Ark
eBay India: MOSQUITO RACKET kills mosquitoes & flys instantly ...
Find MOSQUITO RACKET kills mosquitoes flys instantly in the Consumer Electronics ,
Electronic Gadgets , Other Electronic Gadgets category on eBay India.
eBay India: MOSQUITO RACKET (item 4421231523 end time 30-Nov-2005 ...
Find MOSQUITO RACKET in the Home, Tools Appliances , Home Appliances , Portable

Slide 102

Research Problems

* What cybergenres exist on the web?

* How can we

- Identify genre automatically?
- Recognize new cybergenre?
- Recognize mixed Genre class instances?

* How important is intent vs use?

* Is there a classification scheme for cybergenre?

Slide 103

Recognizing CyberGenres

* The number of cybergenres is increasing

- Different estimates at well over 1000

* Difficult to identify genre

- Sites have features from multiple genre
- New genre are emerging

* Site *vs* individual pages

Slide 104

Potential Page Features

Content

Meta tags

phone numbers

Vocabulary

Form

Number of images.

URL

Size of file in bytes.

Number of words in the page

Structures (tables, lists, paragraphs, etc).

Functionality

Number and type of Links (internal *vs* external)

E-mail Links

Form

Scripts

Slide 105

Automatic Genre Detection

* **1st attempt -> Home pages**
- Personal
- Corporate
- Organization

* **2nd Attempt -> Task**
- Health
- Shopping
- Education

Slide 106

1st Trial

* Automatic Identification of home pages
  – Personal
  – Corporate
  – Organizational

Slide 107

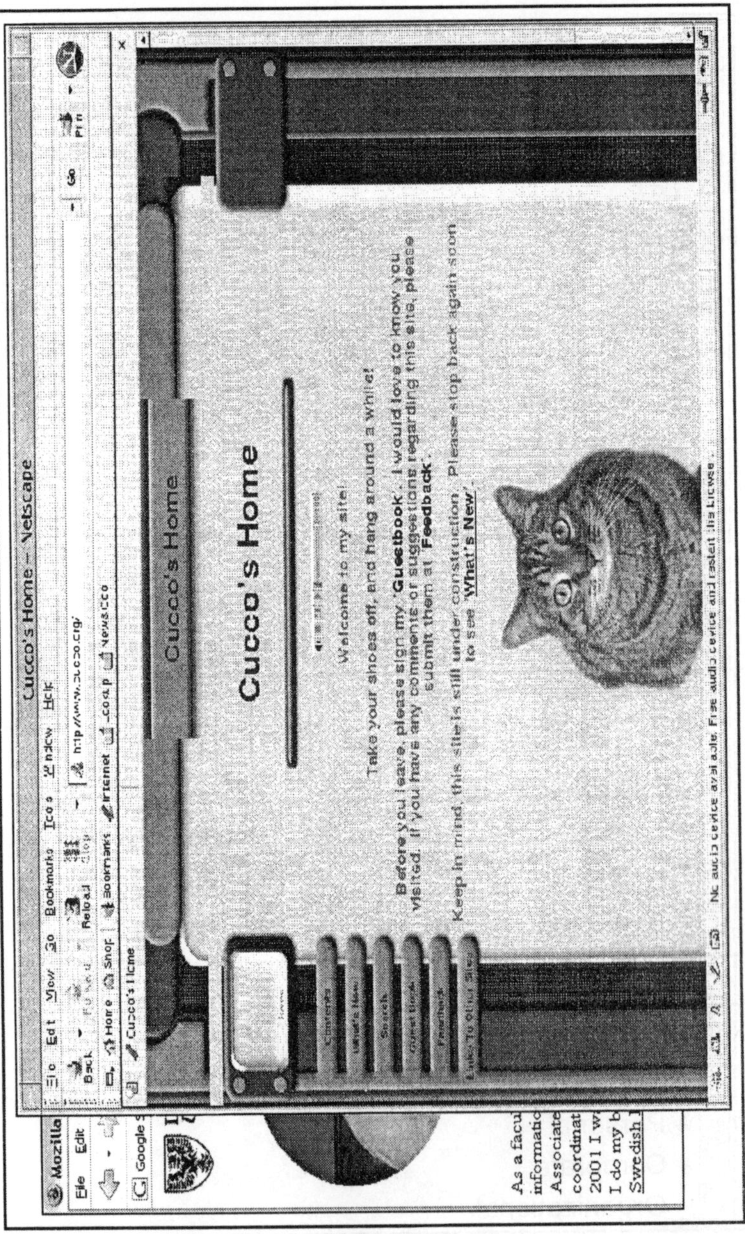
Cucco's Home
Welcome to my site!
Take your shoes off, and hang around a while!
Before you leave, please sign my 'Guestbook'. I would love to know you visited. If you have any comments or suggestions regarding this site, please submit them at 'Feedback'.
Keep in mind, this site is still under construction. Please stop back again soon to see 'What's New'.

Slide 108

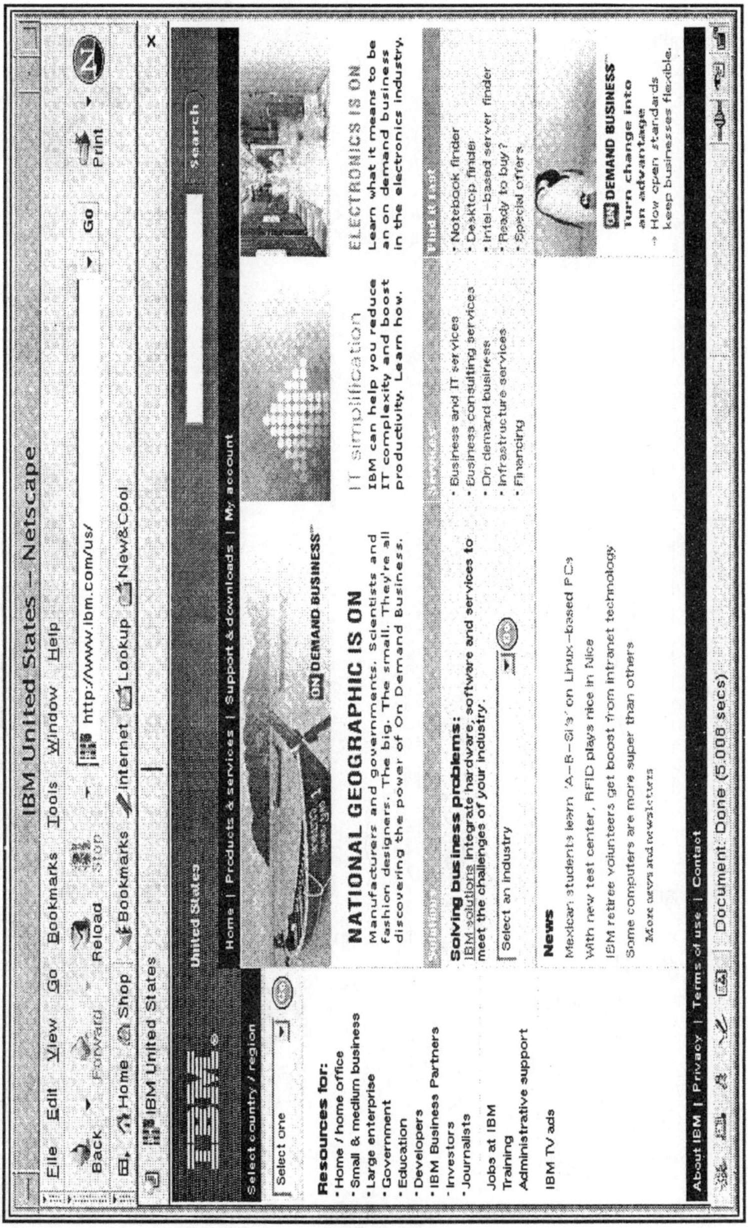
IBM United States – Netscape
File Edit View Go Bookmarks Tools Window Help
Back Forward Reload Stop
http://www.ibm.com/us/
Go
Print
Home Shop Bookmarks Internet Lookup New&Cool
IBM United States
IBM
United States
Home | Products & services | Support & downloads | My account
Search
Select country / region
Select one
Resources for:
· Home / home office
· Small & medium business
· Large enterprise
· Government
· Education
· Developers
· IBM Business Partners
· Investors
· Journalists
Jobs at IBM
Training
Administrative support
IBM TV ads
ON DEMAND BUSINESS
NATIONAL GEOGRAPHIC IS ON
Manufacturers and governments. Scientists and fashion designers. The big. The small. They're all discovering the power of On Demand Business.
IT simplification
IBM can help you reduce IT complexity and boost productivity. Learn how.
ELECTRONICS IS ON
Learn what it means to be an on demand business in the electronics industry.
Solutions
Solving business problems:
IBM solutions integrate hardware, software and services to meet the challenges of your industry.
Select an industry
Services
· Business and IT services
· Business consulting services
· On demand business
· Infrastructure services
· Financing
Find it fast
· Notebook finder
· Desktop finder
· Intel-based server finder
· Ready to buy?
· Special offers
News
Mexican students learn 'A-B-Si's' on Linux-based PCs
With new test center, RFID plays nice in Nice
IBM retiree volunteers get boost from intranet technology
Some computers are more super than others
More news and newsletters
ON DEMAND BUSINESS
Turn change into an advantage
→ How open standards keep businesses flexible.
About IBM | Privacy | Terms of use | Contact
Document: Done (5.008 secs)

Slide 109

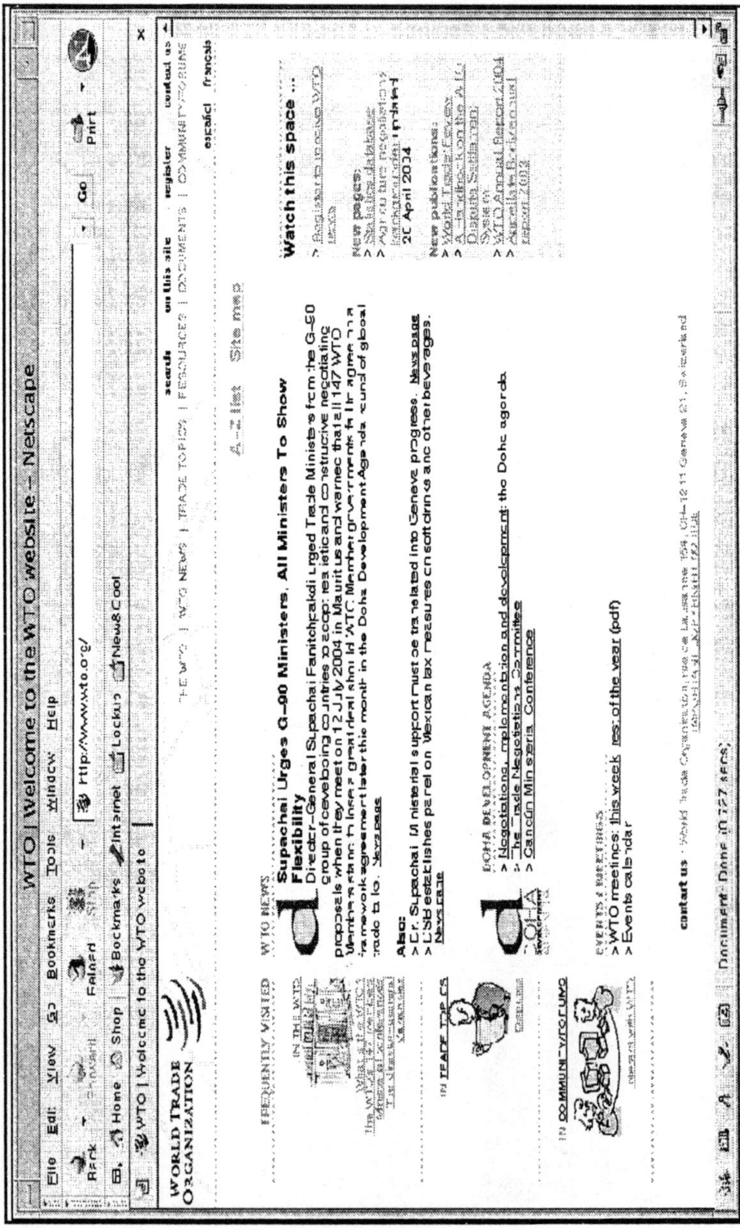
WTO | Welcome to the WTO website - Netscape
WORLD TRADE ORGANIZATION
Supachai Urges G-90 Ministers, All Ministers To Show Flexibility
Watch this space ...

Slide 110

Content Features Used	
Class	**Terms**
Personal Home Page	my, me, i, t
Corporate Home Page	we, services, service, available, fax, our, us, com, contact, copyright, free, amp
Organization Home Page	events, community, organization, 2004, help, its, members, news, information

Slide 111

Results

* separate home pages from noise pages
* separate personal home pages from corporate and organization home pages
* but <u>not</u> between corporate and organizational home pages
* Feature set needs a lot more attention paid to it

Slide 112

2nd Trial: Task and Genre

* Relationship of genre to task
  - Education
* Papers / reports
* Topic web sites
  - Shopping
* Catalog / brochure
* Consumer reports
  - Health
* Medical reports
* Treatment sites

Slide 113

Yahoo Directory

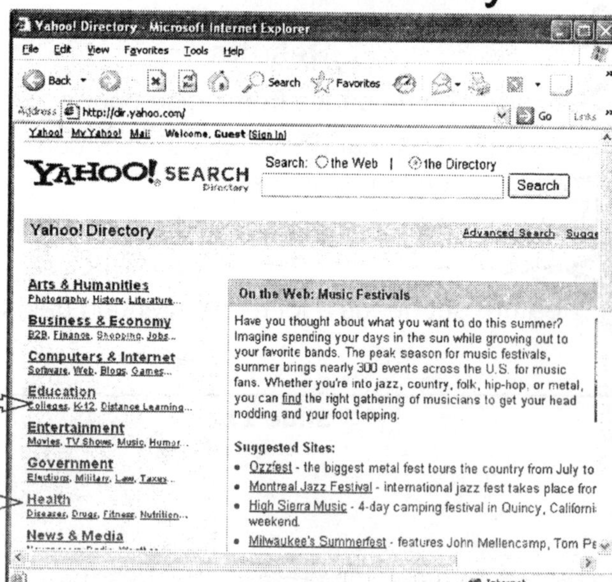

Slide 114

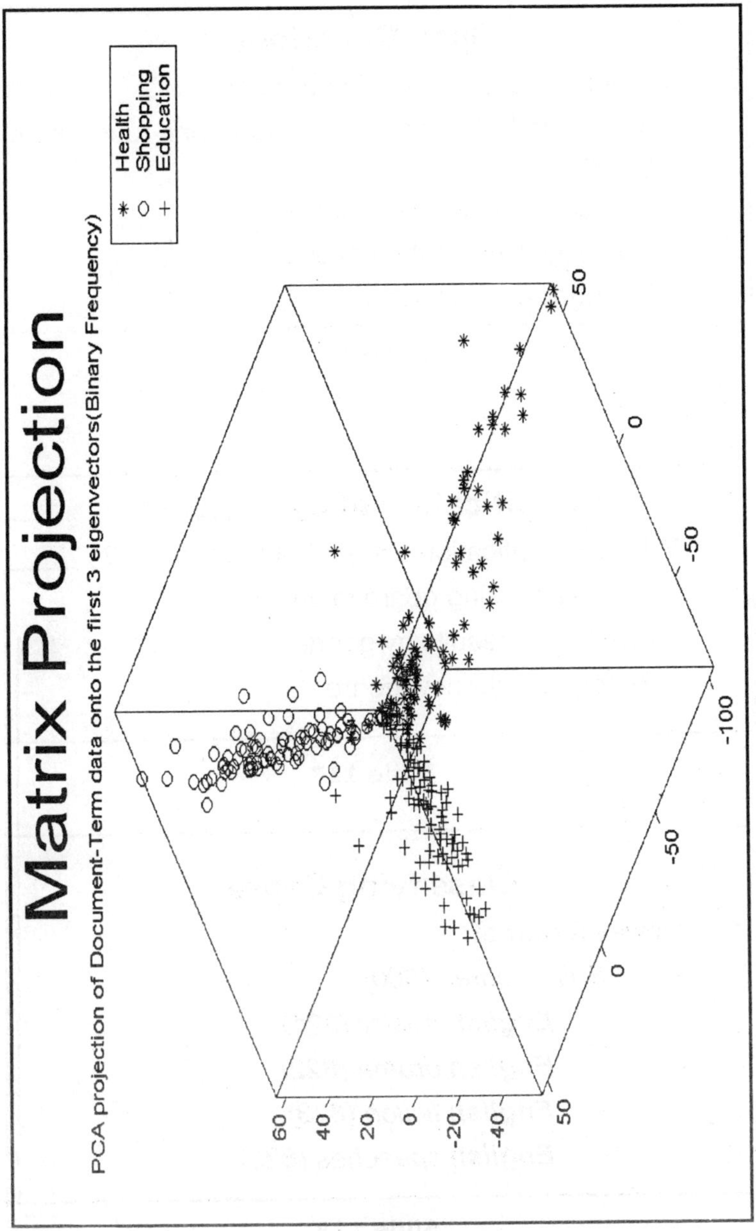
Matrix Projection
PCA projection of Document-Term data onto the first 3 eigenvectors(Binary Frequency)
Health
Shopping
Education
60
40
20
0
-20
-40
50
0
-50
-100
-50
0
50

Slide 115

Open Questions

- * What is an appropriate feature set?
- * What is the potential for using form and functionality features?
- * Need for an Adaptive Schema
  - Track genres as they evolve
  - Recognize novel genre

Slide 116

Classification of Cybergenre

- * Why a classification scheme of cybergenre?
  - Searching using genre in query
  - Categorize results by genre
  - Recognition of new genre

Slide 117

Classifying Genre

- * Dewey **Decimal**
  - — *Belles lettres (800)*
    - – ***English** poetry (821)*
    - – ***English** drama (822)*
    - – ***English** fiction (823)*
    - – ***English** speeches (825)*

Slide 118

GSAFD Genre Terms
A Project of OCLC Research
OCLC
Repository Identification | Table of Contents
Table of Contents
Adventure fiction
Adventure films
Adventure radio programs
Adventure television programs
Allegories
Alternative histories (Fiction)
Animated films
Animated television programs
Arthurian romances
Autobiographical fiction
Bible fiction
Bible films
Bible plays
Bildungsromans
Biographical fiction
Biographical films
Biographical radio programs
Biographical television programs

Slide 119

The Library of Congress >> Especially for Researchers >> Research Centers

Recorded Sound Reference Center

MOTION PICTURE, BROADCASTING & RECORDED SOUND DIVISION

Home >> Guides & Reference Aids >> Radio Form/Genre Terms Guide

Find in Recorded Sound Web Pages go

Examples of Form/Genre and Subject Coding in MARC and non-MARC Settings

Note: RADFG is the code used in USMARC bibliographic records to indicate terms from this list; LCL refers to the Library of Congress local catalog; STAR refers to M/B/RS non-MARC, recorded sound catalog

THE ED SULLIVAN SHOW
LCL: 655 #7 $a Variety $v Television. $2 radfg
650 #0 $a Popular music $y 1961-1970.
STAR: Form/Genre Variety--Television |a MBRS
Form/Genre Popular music--1961-1970 |a LCSH

SPACE LAUNCH PRESS CONFERENCE
LCL: 655 #7 $a Press conferences $v Radio. $2 radfg
610 10 $a Project Mercury (U.S.)
STAR: Form/Genre Press conferences--Radio |a MBRS
Corp subj. Project Mercury (U.S.)

MASS LAUNCHING OF SHIPS IN MAINE (including speeches)
LCL: 655 #7 $a Special events coverage $v Radio. $2 radfg
655 #7 $a Addresses $v Radio. $2 radfg
650 #0 $a Shipbuilding $z Maine.
STAR: Form/Genre Special events coverage--Radio |a MBRS
Form/Genre Addresses--Radio |a MBRS
Topic. subj. Shipbuilding--Maine

Slide 120

Defining a Classification for CyberGenre

* How?
  - Based on a theory (like Atomic table)
  - Based on practice and use
  - Hierarchical or multidimensional

Slide 121

Multidimensional or Hierarchical?

* Hierarchical
  - Top **down approach**
  - **Start with genre in printed medium**
  - **Problems**
    — Single organizational principle
    — Evolution and changing use of documents
* Multidimensional
  - **Bottom up approach**
  - **Consider attributes and use patterns**
  - **Problems**
    — Vocabulary usage
    — Different communities using same genre different purposes

Slide 122

Genre Hierarchies

* Report
  - Scholarly article
  - White paper
  - Text book
  - Popular press
* Novel
  - Detective
  - Western
  - Family saga
* Home page
  - Personal
  - Corporate
  - Organization

Slide 123

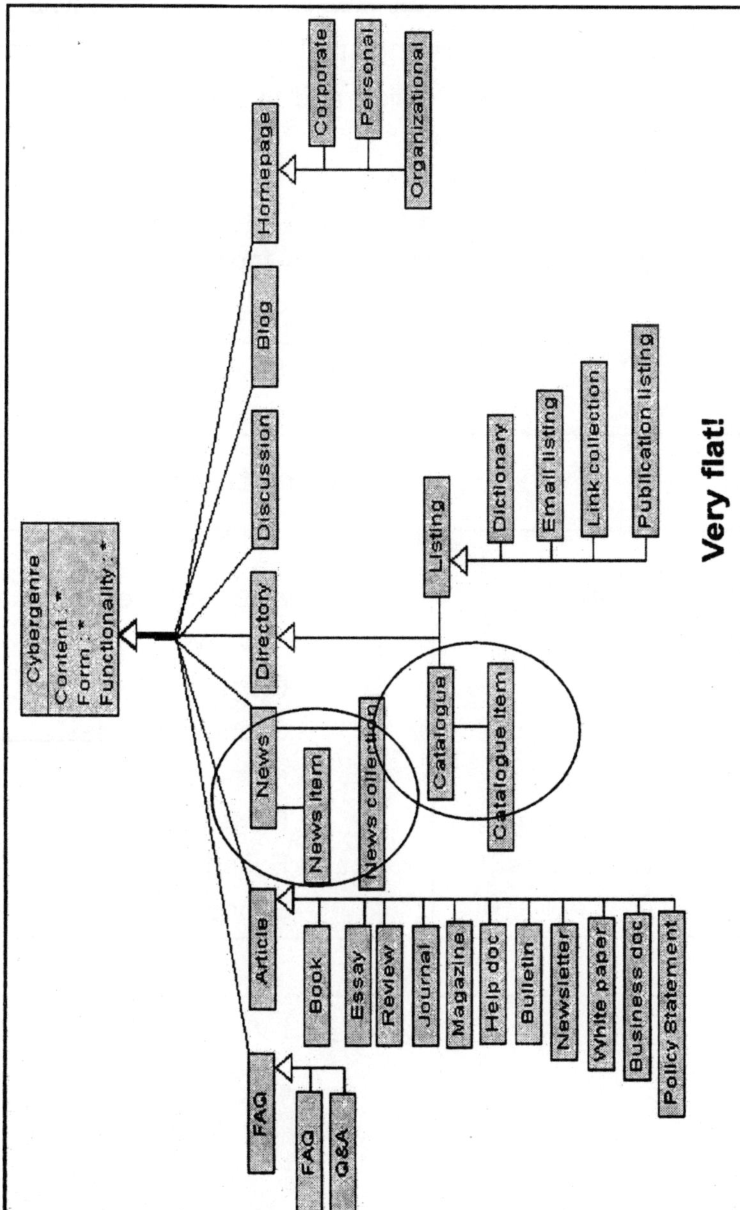
Cybergenre
Content : *
Form : *
Functionality : *
Homepage
Corporate
Personal
Organizational
Blog
Discussion
Directory
Listing
Dictionary
Email listing
Link collection
Publication listing
News
News item
News collection
Catalogue
Catalogue item
Article
Book
Essay
Review
Journal
Magazine
Help doc
Bulletin
Newsletter
White paper
Business doc
Policy Statement
FAQ
FAQ
Q&A
Very flat!

Slide 124

Orthogonality

* Are genre classification and subject classification orthogonal?
  - Finn and Kushmerick (2003)
* Features identified by automatic genre detection algorithms are at least partially topic dependent

Slide 125

Two Level Approach to Use

By Subject	By Genre/Type
– Medicine	– Reviews
– Sports	– Blogs
– Science	– Scholarly articles
– Politics	– Home pages
– Entertainment	– News
– Computers	– Editorial articles
	– Sports scores

Slide 126

Identifying Genre

* By defining individual genre types
    - Lexical and punctuation cues (Karlgren et al, 1994)
    - Syntactic cues (POS & tags) (Stamatatos, 2000)
    - Keywords etc.
* By attributes
    - Identify genre based on attributes and relationships rather than as atomic entities

Slide 127

Examples of CyberGenre Attributes

* **Content**
    - Keywords / Subject Terms / Meta data
    - Images
    - Source
    - Date
* **Form**
    - Structure and layout
    - Style (title, abstract, references, etc)
    - Language level
    - Length
    - Data types (images, numeric tables, maps, etc)
* **Purpose**
    - Author perspective
    - Intended audience
* **Functionality**
    - JavaScript
    - Dynamic data access
    - Links
    - Communication (email, blog, discussion, etc)

Slide 128

Genre Attributes as Facets

Genre::=(Content, Form, Functionality, Purpose)

* <u>Content</u>::= (topic, source, date)
* <u>Form</u>::= (Style, layout, length)
* <u>Functionality</u>::= (Navigation, data access, data input)
* <u>Purpose</u>::= (audience, task)

** represented as <u>Name-value pairs</u>, eg. Topic=::"chemistry"

Slide 129

Slide 130

Genre in Search

* Genre as query attribute

- India mosquito [genre::educational]

* Order results by genre

- Research Articles
- Personal Pages
- Catalog

Slide 131

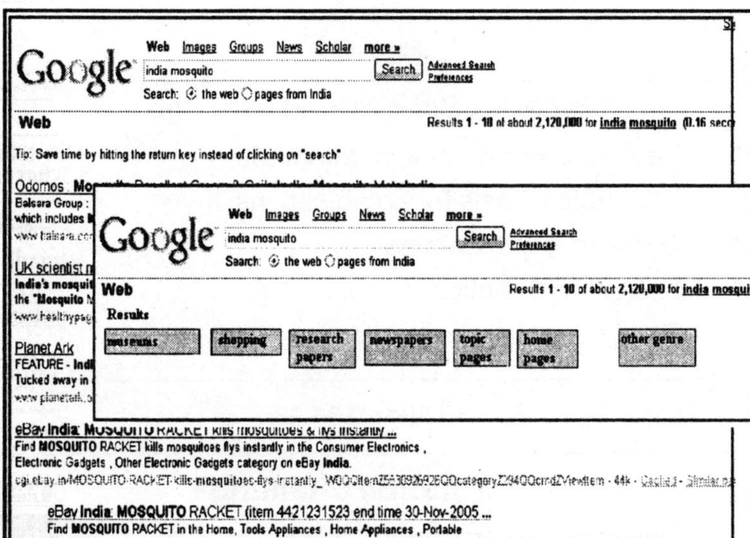

Slide 132

Usefulness of genre??

* Meyer and Stein (2004)
  - Shop
  - Home page
  - Download
  - Discussion
  - Article
  - Link collection
  - Help
* 64% found genre classification useful
* 29% sometimes useful

Slide 133

Faceted Scheme Advantage

* Flexible combinations of attributes
* Theoretical basis for combinations
* Dynamic combinations
* Robust to evolution
* Rationale to choices made

Slide 134

Information Challenge

* Develop classification of genre
  - extensible and robust
  - is interoperable with subject description

Slide 135

... and finally

* This is an exciting research area with the potential of directly effecting web organization and web searching effectiveness!

Slide 136

References

* (Aula et al., 2005)
* **Brown and Sellen**, 2005
* **Barreau, D.**, **Nardi, B.A.** (1995). Finding and Reminding: File Organization from the Desktop, SIGCHI Bulletin, July 1995, 27(3):39-43.
* **Bellotti, V., Ducheneaut, N., Howard, M., and Smith, I.** (2003). Taking Email to Task: The Design and Evaluation of a Task Management Centered Email Tool, In Proc. of SIGCHI 2003 Conference on Human Factors in Computing Systems, Fort Lauderdale Florida, April 2003, 345-352.
* Card et al., 1996
* Catledge and Pitkow, 1995
* Choo et al., 2000
* Dumais et al., 2003
* Jhaveri et al. 2005
* Jones et al., 2001
* Kellar et al., 2005
* Malone, 1983
* Mander, Saloman, Wong, 1992
* Sellen et al. 2002
* Whittaker and Sidner, 1996

Slide 137

Keeping Things Found

* Keeping Found Things Found (KFTF) for management of re-use of information *(Jones et al., 2001)*
  - access information from anywhere
  - notification of updates or deletion of information
  - reminding function
  - integration with existing information collections
  - easy to share and maintenance of information

Slide 138

Browser Examples

* WebBook and WebForager (Card et al., 1996)
* WebClippings (Sellen et al. 2002)
* Session Highlights *(Jhaveri et al. 2005)*

Slide 139

Genre & Boundary Objects

* Objects that connect and define communities of use
* News pages
  - General public
  - Advertisers
  - Students
  - Finance workers
* Home pages
  - Self and family
  - Communities of like interest, etc rock collectors
* Research pages in Health
  - Researchers
  - Patients
  - Practitioners
  - Administrators

Slide 140

Subjective Categorization of CyberGenre

Genre	C&W 1997	Dewe etal 1998	S&W 1998
Homepage	10%	12%	40%
Resource	82%	44%	35%
Catalog & Brochure	8%	17%	22%
Discussion		12%	
News			
FAQ		5%	
Dictionary		11%	
Entertainment	0%		3%

Slide 141

Index